TDC

The Dynamic Church

Author - O.J. Gibson
Editorial Assistance - Erich Wiegar
Technical Assistance - Roger Rayhbuck

Produced as a service to the Lord's people by Fairhaven Ministries, an outreach of Fairhaven Bible Chapel, 401 MacArthur Blvd., San Leandro, California. Fairhaven Bible Chapel is an independent, autonomous, New Testament church dedicated to evangelism and discipleship through the matrix of local churches (Matthew 28:19,20; Acts 2:42).

Walterick Publishers
P.O. Box 2216
Kansas City, KS 66110-0216

PREFACE

Why a course on the church?

Because of the importance given to this subject by the Lord Jesus, our God and Savior.

Because of its divinely assigned role as the pillar and ground of the truth in the world (1 Tim. 3:15).

Because its lack (where the church is not established) is a disaster, or its weaknesses and failures are crippling disabilities to the work of God.

Because the lack of understanding or appreciation in many quarters undermines its proper support and function.

Because its Biblical principles of function have been confused and obscured by centuries of distortion, disobedience, neglect, compromise, expediency, and indifference to divine order. Modern churches often claim to follow the Bible alone, but do not seem to model what we read in its pages. The argument that something was merely cultural or local and not binding is freely used to excuse this contradiction.

This course cannot perfectly cover all issues or please every point of view. Its purpose is to review major principles relating to a Biblical church, and consider the question, "What says the Scriptures?" That is not the same thing as saying, "What is the view of Luther, Calvin, or some other leader?" Nor, "What do the creeds and councils say?" Nor, "What helps increase numerical growth as proven by surveys?"

Quotations from Scripture will be used to establish points--as well as possible in a limited space. The New Testament records the beginning of the church of the Lord Jesus Christ with instruction or examples needed to regulate it.

Please read each lesson thoughtfully. In sections where it may seem wrong to you, please be patient and do not let this deter you from considering the remainder of the material. Where it is evidently right, ask yourself if you are following its principles faithfully, true to Christ the Head.

The Lord of the church will soon return to evaluate what we have done in the church in His Name. *Maranatha!*

HOW TO GET THE MOST OUT OF THIS COURSE

Your study of "The Dynamic Church" will be the most profitable if you give heed to the following guidelines for personal preparation and class participation.

PERSONAL PREPARATION BEFORE CLASS

Set aside adequate time each week for the completion of your homework. You should take the following steps for each lesson:

1. PRAY TO GOD. Ask Him to help you understand and apply His word. Let your prayer be: "Open Thou mine eyes, that I may behold wondrous things out of THY law." (Psalm 119:18).

2. READ THE NOTES. Underline important thoughts and anything that you do not understand, or about which you have questions. Look up key Scripture references and read them from a modern translation.

3. ANSWER THE STUDY GUIDE QUESTIONS. After reading the notes, complete all items of the study guide. If you have difficulty with a question, pass on to the next question and return later to the troublesome question.

AUTHOR'S NOTE: The terms *church* and/or *assembly* can be used interchangeably for the purpose of this study.

TABLE OF CONTENTS

LESSON/TITLE/DESCRIPTION   PAGE

THE IMPORTANCE AND DEFINITION
OF THE CHURCH   LESSON 1

"I will build my church... " (Matt. 16:18)

This remarkable statement of purpose by the Lord Jesus Christ shows us that the Church is a divine institution of the greatest significance. The Lord purposed to replace the nation of Israel, then representing God on earth, with an entirely new community. The Israelites were to be a light to the nations so that God's salvation could reach to the ends of the earth (Isa. 42:6). As His chosen people, Israel was unfaithful to God in this sacred mission. Its holy city, priesthood, temple and sacrificial system were wiped out. Its own prophets had repeatedly cautioned about judgment, but it was in vain.

God raised up a new body, without any distinction between Jew and Gentile (Col. 3:11; Eph. 2:11-18). The Hebrew prophets had foreseen a worldwide ministry among the nations. They also prophesied the setting aside of Israel because of unbelief and spiritual unfaithfulness. The truth of the church as God's people, was a mystery in former days until revealed in the New Testament (Eph. 3:4,5). The church was still a future development before the time period of the four Gospels and the first chapter of Acts. Its formation occurred for the first time on the Jewish Feast of Pentecost (Acts 2) by the initial action of incorporating believers into Christ, called *the baptism of the Spirit* (Acts 1:5; 1 Cor. 12:12,13). The Church is not a continuation of Israel, but rather succeeds it. The Church now functions for God in the interval of Israel's national rejection by God (Rom. 11:1,2). In the future a believing remnant of Israel will be restored to God through the Lord Jesus Christ, whom the nation now rejects (Rom. 11:25,26; Zech. 12:10; 13:1). God now calls people to Christ through the witness of His Church. He adds to that Church daily those who are being saved (Acts 2:47).

God established His Church for His purposes. Believers are not saved to live in a solitary or individualistic relationship with God as some are prone to believe. They are called to fellowship in spiritual communities as functioning members of God's family. God says they are not to forsake assembling together (Heb. 10:25). The Church is a divinely ordained body and deserves respect, support and personal involvement by all of God's people. No devout Israelite would have ignored his responsibilities in the spiritual life of his community. Similarly, no devout Christian should be indifferent to the Church as his or her spiritual family.

IDENTIFYING THE CHURCH

What is the church? Some think of it as a building in which meetings are held (*"the church at the corner"*). Some speak of it in terms of a denomination or religious organization (*"To what church do you belong?"*). The Scriptural meaning, on a local level, is *a congregation of believers in Christ who gather to worship, pray, study the Word of God, and observe the ordinances* (baptism and the Lord's Supper). In truth, the Church goes into a building rather than the people go into the church.

The word *church* is a poor choice for translating the meaning of the Greek *ekklesia*. The common, ordinary, and reasonable translation is that of an assembly or congregation. The word means a called-out or called-together company. In itself it is not a religious term. In the New Testament it is used to describe the Ephesians in a theater (Acts 19:32,41), and the wandering Israelites in the wilderness (Acts 7:38). When applied to the assembly of believers in the Lord Jesus, it refers to their gathering in the name of the Lord (2 Thess. 2:1; 1 Cor. 5:4). It is a particular kind of assembly that is in view, God's people gathered to the Name of Jesus. It is a people alive in Christ, congregating in a spiritual sense.

TWO VIEWS OF THE CHURCH

The word Church is used both in a general or universal sense as well as in a local sense.

The **universal church** includes all true believers in Christ, both those who are now with Christ and those yet living. It includes the period from the day of Pentecost to the Rapture. Ephesians 1:22,23 speaks of Christ being the Head over all things to the Church, which is His Body. Other references in Ephesians 3:10,21 and 5:23-32 or Colossians 1:18,24 also focus on the Church as a unity of all believers under Christ's headship. No unsaved people are in it, and no saved people are outside of it. To date, the entire Church has not been gathered together in one place at one time. Such will be the case, however, when Christ returns and unites them all (1 Thess. 4:14-17). This description should make clear why no earthly church should make the preposterous claim that it is in itself that one true church. No earthly church is identical with the universal and true Church. We are one with all true believers and unified in Christ's Church.

The **local church (or churches)** has to do with the gatherings of born-again believers in a locality. Many of the New Testament letters are written to such churches. Rome, Corinth, Ephesus, Philippi, Colossae and Thessalonica are examples. Letters to Timothy concern the organization and leadership of local churches. Titus came to join Paul on the island of Crete to appoint elders for local churches. Paul's task as a missionary was to establish local churches where none existed, even if Jewish synagogues functioned there. It is fair to say that the New Testament does not contemplate believers who are not associated with a local church. Expressions like "churches of Christ," "churches of God," "churches of Galatia," or of "Macedonia" or "Judea" define local congregations in terms of the Lord's Name or of a locality. No sectarian names are used. Forming groups or naming churches after men is forbidden and erroneous (1 Cor. 1:12,13). A local church ideally should: (1) have functioning elders and deacons who are shepherding and taking responsibility for the spiritual care of those whom God has placed in their care (1 Cor. 16:16; Heb. 13:17), (2) be practicing the two ordinances of the church: baptism (Matt. 28:19,20; Acts 2:41,42) and the Lord's Supper (1 Cor. 11:23-26), and (3) provide an environment in which believers can exercise their spiritual gifts for mutual edification (Heb. 10:25; 1 Cor. 14:26).

One cannot understand how any Biblically informed believer can think it is not necessary to be a functioning part of a local church. Non-participation, non-support or neglect of the gatherings of God's people is unthinkable for one who would truly claim to follow and obey the Lord Jesus, the Head of the Church. To abandon voluntarily church participation, after once attending, is to place one in questionable company (1 John 2:19). Listening to radio broadcasts and worship at home may be necessary for invalids, other shut-ins, and isolated believers. Radio and television may act as helpful tools of evangelism and Bible teaching. However, if we allow the so-called "electronic church" to keep us from participating in the local church, practicing its ordinances, and being spiritually accountable to its leaders (Heb. 13:17), then we have erred. We should not allow so-called parachurch organizations to ever become a substitute for the local church.

NAMES FOR THE CHURCH

Biblical names for the church are instructive. A variety of such names are used for the assembly. They apply to all believers. None are used in a sectarian way. These include:

1. **Church of God** (1 Cor. 10:32; 15:9), indicating divine ownership.

2. **Church of Christ** (Rom. 16:16), indicating its relationship to the Founder.

3. **Bride of Christ** (Eph. 5:25-27; 2 Cor. 11:2), indicating the loving relationship and commitment of the Lord to His own.

4. **Body of Christ** (Eph. 1:22,23), illustrating the way in which the Lord expresses His life through His members.

5. **Temple of God** (1 Cor. 3:16), showing that it is the dwelling of the Holy Spirit; also that we as holy priests are "living stones," brought together as a holy house of worship (1 Pet. 2:5).

6. **Flock of God** (John 10:16), illustrating that we are the sheep of Christ of which He is the Great Shepherd (Heb. 13:20; 1 Pet. 2:25).

7. **House of God** (1 Tim. 3:15), suggesting that the order and discipline appropriate to that over which the Lord presides.

This list may not be complete, but is adequate to suggest two things. First, they all relate the Lord's people to none other than Himself. Second, they do not divide from one another the entirety of believers in any way. They enable all believers to relate to one another in an unrestricted way on the ground of the blood of Christ. Like David then, we can be a companion of all those who fear the Lord and of those who keep His precepts (Psa. 119:63).

NAMES FOR CHURCH MEMBERS

Our primary membership is in the Body of Christ, not a religious organization. The common denominational names for church members, so often deemed essential, are not used in the Bible to identify believers. Instead, names are given which are appropriate to all who are in Christ and that worship our only Lord and Savior in truth.

1. The term **Believers** (Acts 5:14) indicates the channel of faith by which we enter the Kingdom of God and continue to relate to Him in life.

2. The name **Disciples** (Acts 9:1) describes imitating and following the Lord Jesus by those who profess to be His followers; they are adherents or practitioners of His teaching.

3. The title **Saints** (Eph. 1:1) means "holy ones" and shows our separation unto God and from defilement according to our position as being "in Christ."

4. The name **Brethren** (Jas. 2:1) indicates the family relationship among members of God's family as brothers and sisters in Christ.

5. The term **Christians** (Acts 11:26) is the least common name denoting our relationship to Christ and was used primarily by unbelievers in Biblical times to describe the faithful.

IDENTIFYING A SCRIPTURAL CHURCH

It is very difficult for people throughout the world to understand the varieties of churches which call themselves Christian. Many, if not most of them, do not present a message which is faithful to the Gospel or to other major Scriptural truths. Even believers are often confused. The following warnings should be given.

True and false churches operate side by side in many places. This underscores the truth that there have always been true and false prophets or teachers and true and false believers. We must be taught to distinguish the one from the other. The Lord taught the parable of the wheat and tares to illustrate this principle (Matt. 13:24-30,36-43). He paralleled this teaching with the parable of the good fish and bad (Matt. 13:47-50). "Not everyone that says Lord, Lord, shall enter the Kingdom," said the Lord Jesus, "but he who does the will of My Father who is in Heaven" (Matt. 7:21-23).

How can we know the difference between the true and the false? We ought to know them by their fruits, or evidences of reality (Matt. 7:16).

Do they clearly proclaim or teach the Gospel message of salvation and call upon people to repent, believe, and be born again? Or do they leave the people with the wrong impression that church membership, baptism, and rituals will save them at the end? Do they emphasize God's word as the final authority in matters of faith and practice? Or do they refer to human authority and tradition as equally acceptable as a guide (Matt. 15:3,9)? Is it the Lord Himself or some latter-day prophet and human organization that has the final say? Does the church glorify Christ or some earthly leader? Does the church nurture its people through the study of the Word of God or through human theories? Is it concerned about bringing the unsaved heathen multitudes to know Christ, or is it apathetic to the world's spiritual needs? Do the lives of the leaders bear clear evidence of moral transformation by the power of God's Spirit, or are they merely pursuing a career in ministry? These and other questions should help make the distinction between "the spirit of truth and the spirit of error" (1 John 4:6).

Racial or state churches have arisen to represent Christ and His Kingdom. It is understandable that those of similar culture and language will want to come together for worship. However, this has led many to identify with a church solely because of cultural reasons or community pressure. At times these churches have drifted far from a Biblical foundation. Many have imposed a hierarchy of priests and officials separating the people from direct worship of the Lord. Their followers do not study the Word for themselves. They depend on the teaching of their professionally trained and ordained leaders as their authority. National churches tend to develop this pattern, using culture and tradition, rather than

10

Scriptural principles, as a guide.

A church may come together as a community of the same language. Yet in God's eyes there can be no racial or state church as His one church. There is no basis for such a separation. "Is Christ divided?" (1 Cor. 1:13). We are all one in Christ Jesus. There is one Body, one Spirit, one hope, one Lord, one faith, one baptism, one God (Eph. 4:4,5). We will not sit in heaven as separated racial, language, or cultural groups.

The situation is made worse when the state and the church are merged, which historically has been a disaster for the cause of Christ. Furthermore, this merger has no Biblical authority. People tend to depend upon their association with a state, or any church, as their hope of heaven, rather than on a personal relationship with Christ. They are caught up in the thinking and teaching of their group, not what Scripture teaches. This condition is made worse when the church itself does not teach or practice the truths of God's Word. It gives the members false hopes that through such things as infant baptism and participation in sacraments, they will be accepted by God.

GOD'S PLAN FOR THE CHURCH

The Church is a part of the determined counsel of God from eternity past. It occupies the mind of the Lord today. It will be prominent even in the ages to come (Eph. 2:7). If Christ is Head, Chief Cornerstone, and Central Figure, how could it be anything but vitally important (Eph. 2:20-22)? To be ignorant of the true nature of the Church is to be ignorant of what is central to the plans of our Lord in His past, present and future activities.

It was God's eternal purpose, before the foundation of the world, that His wisdom be displayed through the Church to the rulers and authorities in the heavenly realms (Eph. 3:10,11). He planned that the Church would reflect His holy character. He saved and called His people to a holy life, reflecting His character and ways. Even the very "living stones" of God's Church were chosen in Him before the foundation of the world (Eph. 1:4). The Church is not an alternate plan or afterthought of God. It was on His heart from the beginning.

1. THE PURCHASER

Known also to God from the beginning was the awful cost involved in establishing the Church (1 Pet. 1:19,20). Christ purchased it with His own blood (Acts 20:28b). He laid down His life for His sheep (John 10:15). The Church was the pearl of great price, which when He found it, He gave all that He had for it (Matt. 13:46). This teaching about Christ's death, burial, and resurrection on behalf of the Church was to be the essence of the Gospel (1 Cor. 15:3,4).

What a marvel it should be to us, His church, that Christ gave Himself to be the Foundation, the Chief Cornerstone and the Divine Indweller of His glorious church (Col. 1:27; 1 Cor. 3:11). How can we be indifferent toward that for which Christ paid so much?

2. THE PREPARER

Christ personally selected and trained the first church leaders, the Apostles. However, it is the common practice of some to look at Jesus' three years of ministry (the gospel period) as being completely detached from the Church Age that follows it in the book of Acts. For what did Christ train these men? In Matthew, the Great Commission comes at the end of the Gospel (Matt. 28:18-20), but in Acts it comes as a preface to the story of the early church (Acts 1:8). Thus the last command in the Gospels was the first command in the Acts.

3. THE BUILDER

Christ said that He would build His Church. It is true that He works through the Holy Spirit as His representative to the Church. However, a look at the book of Acts reveals also the direct, personal involvement of the Lord Jesus, the Head of the Church. The Lord Himself adds to the Church those who are being saved (Acts 2:47b). He places the *living stones* into His building (1 Pet. 2:5). The Lord Himself told Ananias that Saul (Paul) was to be, "...a chosen instrument of **Mine**, to bear **My** name before the Gentiles and Kings and the sons of Israel. For I will show him how much he must suffer for **My** name's sake" (Acts 9:15,16).

4. THE OVERSEER

Not only is Christ the builder who is directly involved in selecting the materials and the laborers, but He is also the overseer of each local church. In the book of Revelation, Christ is seen standing among the seven lampstands, which represent seven actual churches located in Asia existing in the first century. In His message to each church, Christ indicates His concern and involvement with every one of them. They are directly responsible to Him.

Christ personally identifies with the Church. To touch the Church is to touch the heart of Christ. When Saul was breathing out murderous threats against the infant Church, Christ confronted him, "Saul, Saul, why do you persecute **Me**?" Saul was not sure who the Lord was. "Who are you, Lord?" Saul asked. "I am Jesus, whom you are persecuting," He replied.

CONCLUSION AND APPLICATION

The Lord Jesus entered into a mighty undertaking when He came to save His people from their sins. However, He did not limit His work to saving individuals. He lovingly made provision for them to be brought into a spiritual community, His own assembly. This community, called His Body, is to function through gathering centers in every locality where the Gospel goes forth. Where the message is preached, churches necessarily will be established where God's people can gather. They should be Biblically sound and spiritually healthy.

Local churches are not simply a means to an end, just one among many helpful things the Lord ordained. They are the central focus of Christ's purposes on earth.

The Dynamic Church
STUDY GUIDE

THE IMPORTANCE AND DEFINITION OF THE CHURCH
LESSON 1

1. What is the definition of the word **church**?

2. When did the church begin, and how was it formed?

3. What is the difference between the universal church and local churches?

4. Give **two** reasons you would use to answer a person who says, "I don't believe you need to go to church to live a Christian life."

5. Give **three** ways in which you can distinguish a true church from a false one.

6. What name (or names) would you use to identify yourself as a follower of the Lord Jesus? State why.

7. OPINION: State one truth in this lesson which most impressed you.

8. Do you have any unanswered questions on material covered in this lesson?

The Dynamic Church
NOTES

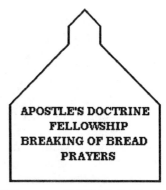

APOSTLE'S DOCTRINE
FELLOWSHIP
BREAKING OF BREAD
PRAYERS

THE PURPOSE OF THE CHURCH   LESSON 2

"To Him be the glory in the church and in Christ Jesus to all generations, forever and ever. Amen" (Eph. 3:21).

One cannot correctly answer the question, "What is the purpose of the church?," without first asking, "What is the purpose of my life as a believer?" If you feel free to live according to your own preferences, you will find that it is easy to feel open about whatever way the church functions according to convenience or custom. However, if it is God who works in you both to will and to do for His good pleasure (Phil. 2:13), then your purpose of life will be that of being an obedient disciple. Be a believer who lives with the purpose of pleasing God above every other consideration. This will also guide you in answering the question for yourself, "Why did God establish my local assembly?"

The proper functioning of a spiritual community of believers is an extension of God's purpose for individuals. Together we can do certain things that we cannot do as well, or not at all, as individuals. Therefore, we should not conceive of the church's activities in terms that do not reflect the purpose of God. For example, consider the following descriptions of the local church, and ask yourself how they reflect God's thinking. Is the church an exclusive club for a limited group? Is it a lecture auditorium where we hear good speakers? Is it a center for social work and community development? Is it an entertainment center offering, at times, tickets for admission? Is it a political action center? Is it a kitchen and dining facility for social reasons? If it is none of these, what then is God's purpose for the local church?

1. PICTURES OF OUR PURPOSE

Our purpose together is pictured by three descriptive terms for the church in the book of Ephesians.

A. **The Body of Christ.** It is *His* body and Jesus is the Head (Eph. 1:23). It is *one* body (Eph. 4:4). It is built up by members using their spiritual gifts (Eph. 4:12). Its members are like Christ's flesh and bones (Eph. 5:30). First Corinthians 12:12-27 expounds the function of the members as interdependent and varied.

B. **The Bride of Christ.** This expression is most clearly given in Revelation 21:2,9, but the truth is fully expounded in Ephesians 5:23-32. Christ's love for the church is like the ideal husband's love for a cherished wife. Affection and intimacy are strongly in view. For I am jealous for you with a godly jealousy; for I betrothed you to one husband, that to Christ I might present you as a pure virgin (2 Cor. 11:2).

   C. **The Building of Christ.** The church is built upon the foundation of the apostles and prophets, Jesus Christ Himself being the cornerstone, in whom the whole building, being fitted together, is growing into a holy temple in the Lord...a dwelling place of God in the Spirit (Eph. 2:20-22). As also stated in 1 Peter 2:5, we are living stones, being built up as a spiritual house for a holy priesthood, to offer up spiritual sacrifices acceptable to God through Jesus Christ. The idea of a worshiping community, replacing the literal Temple at Jerusalem, indicates the presence of God in a particular way in the church.

From these illustrations we learn that our purpose as the Church is to build up the people of God, to be in intimate relationship with Christ as a community, and to worship together as holy priests. Is this the way we see ourselves? Is this the way those outside the Church perceive us?

2. THE ESSENCE OF OUR PURPOSE

The local church which has a mission to please the Lord should do these things:

   A. **Glorify God** by representing Him in His holy, loving, and gracious manner before the world. Those outside of Christ should see the magnificent glory of God and His Son in the lives of the people. In a special way, God is glorified through His Son (John 17:1,5). All who honor the Son, honor the Father (John 5:23). Those who display in their lives the moral likeness of the Lord Jesus, and give Him the credit, glorify God. We should show forth the praises of Him who has called us out of darkness into His marvelous light (1 Pet. 2:9). The Church should exhibit the wisdom of God (Eph. 3:10) and the grace of God (Eph. 2:7) extended to us poor sinners who are but specks of dust on one tiny planet in space. Our activities should glorify God. Our lives should reflect His character. Do others see God's glory displayed in us who profess to be His holy people? Will they fall on their faces and worship God, declaring that God is certainly among us (1 Cor. 14:25) because they see His life in us?

   B. **Worship God** in spirit and in truth. That is what the Father seeks (John 4:23,24). We are to worship in spirit an **invisible** God; not idols, images, or material objects said to represent God. We are to worship in truth, according to His plan, remembering His work for us, and the precious blood which was shed to provide the ground of our acceptance. We should worship daily as individuals. We are also called to worship Christ collectively. For this ministry, the first day of the week especially is set apart. Heaven's worship centers on the Lamb that was slain for us (Rev. 5:11-14). It should be done likewise on earth as the assembly worships. The value of worship is seen in that Satan covets it (Matt. 4:9). Angels and devout servants of God refuse it, knowing that it is only for God. Therefore, no church should neglect what is preeminent with God in its own activities.

C. **Obey God** in the Great Commission (Matt. 28:19,20). The commission is called "great" precisely because it exceeds other responsibilities. We are to go and make disciples, baptize them and then teach them to observe everything the Lord commanded. In the power of the Spirit, we are to be His witnesses, beginning at our "Jerusalem" (the immediate community around us) and extending to the most remote part of the world through missionary work (Acts 1:8). Local churches are represented as *lampstands* (Rev. 1:20), indicating a light of testimony to those around them. Israel failed as a light to the nations. As a local church we must not fail in this responsibility. When we are not witnessing fervently as the early church did (Acts 5:42), we have ceased to be the evangelizing force. Ours is a missionary, evangelizing faith. The church is not to be a place of convenient meetings for a select group. If the harvest is plentiful and the laborers are few, we should both pray and work to remedy the deficiency (Matt. 9:37,38). God is concerned about every lost soul (2 Pet. 3:9). How can we justify apathy about a perishing world?

3. THE FULFILLING OF OUR PURPOSE

What happened in the earliest meetings of the local churches? Acts 2:42 says, "And they were continually devoting themselves to the apostles' teaching and to fellowship and to the breaking of bread and to prayer." In other words, they were studying and obeying the Word of God, strengthening one another in spiritual fellowship, observing the Lord's Supper and praying regularly and collectively. We can analyze the purpose of the church in a larger way by utilizing various Scriptures. Acts 2:42 does not exhaust the subject.

A. **Teach God's Word**, in season and out of season, if people are to be delivered from Scriptural malnutrition and ignorance (2 Tim. 4:2). This should involve listening to the whole counsel of God, not simply selected portions (Acts 20:27). The lack of systematic teaching in the whole church community has been a blight for many congregations who only hear random and assorted passages from their leaders who do not feed their souls. An earthly altar was the center of worship in the Old Testament. Our altar, the cross on which the sacrifice of Christ was made, can be seen only through effective teaching and reception of the Word. To hear and obey the Word of God is a mark of those who are heaven bound. It is superior to practicing impressive religious rituals (1 Sam. 15:22). People need more than warm, religious feelings, coming through rituals performed by a priest or minister. They need to be taught the Word of God faithfully, and shown how to study the Word of God by themselves (Acts 17:11).

B. **Shepherd God's People** through spiritual leaders. Both the Lord Jesus and His apostles taught the importance of pastoral leadership (John 21:15-17; 1 Pet. 5:2). This can only be accomplished when people assemble in flocks and are tended by faithful undershepherds of the Great Shepherd. Shepherding involves the loving care of those within the flock, beginning with the new born believer, a babe in Christ (1 Pet. 2:2). The word *babe* applies also to the carnal Christian (1 Cor. 3:1-3), one who remains immature, not growing on the solid food of the Word that should have been applied to his soul (Heb. 5:12-14). Such a person will not live a lawless life, an impossibility for a true believer (1 John 3:4-9). Carnal Christians have never grown out of spiritually infantile behavior. Proper shepherd care helps believers to mature, rather than live childishly in spiritual and emotional behavior. Sheep are commanded to obey their shepherds. They in turn must give account for their souls to the Lord (Heb. 13:17). This presupposes that the sheep have not isolated themselves from churches. Some believers operate as free-floating individualists without a clear commitment to any local church, something for which there is no New Testament sanction. Shepherds of the flock have a serious responsibility for their charges, and failure will be noted by God. Israel's leaders failed in this area and came under divine condemnation (Ezek. 34:2-10). The quality of shepherding care for God's people by elders or pastors will bring them either reward or loss at the Judgment Seat of Christ (1 Pet. 5:4; 1 Cor. 3:13-15).

C. **Fellowship with God's People** in a community gathering, as seen in Acts 2:42. Fellowship in the church is primarily spiritual, not social. It majors on enjoying the presence of the Lord in the midst of His people. It includes speaking to Him in collective prayer and worship. Here we can give thoughtful attention to the preaching or teaching of God's Word. When we forsake the assembling of ourselves together, we are inviting a drift from God and a weakening of spiritual life (Heb. 10:25). It is a serious mistake to lose the stimulus, encouragement, and accountability inherent in an active participation in the life of the assembly. Attending church meetings will not automatically guarantee spirituality by any means. Hypocrites and hearers only also go to meetings. Neglect of church attendance usually signals a downward spiritual course.

D. **Edify God's People** through the mutual function of gifted people. That is why the Lord gave spiritual gifts to His people when He left this earth (Eph. 4:10-12). Such gifts are divine enablements given to each believer to build up others in the fellowship so they can better serve God. Whether it is a speaking gift such as teaching, or a serving gift such as helps or mercy, God's object is to help others, **not** to fulfill personal ambition. Gifted people function like parts of the human body in variety, interdependence, and contribution to the whole (1 Cor. 12). By their very nature they operate in a group setting. The gifts mature as they are used properly, and languish when neglected. Every believer has at least one gift, and all are important to the total functioning of the church. Building up the believers involves training them for service within the church. Certain gifts operate to carry out this function. Training the twelve and others was a great part of the ministry of the Lord while He lived on earth. Training of believers to serve the Lord is as important as training children to live in the world. The New Testament does not present the idea of delegating such training to outside institutions or ministries. Rather, it is a responsibility of the church to provide training for all who wish to learn. There are, of course, certain areas of training which may require specialized help for which the church is not equipped. But as much as possible, the church needs to provide all that is necessary for the healthy growth of each member, including leadership development.

CONCLUSION AND APPLICATION

These considerations should remind us of the broad scope of responsibilities given by God to the local church. The individual believer is called to function as a useful participant in the local Body. This community and its leaders should assume responsibility for the proper care and growth of its members. This includes requiring spiritual cleanliness or holiness for the members. God's purpose is to have a glorious church, not having spot, wrinkle, or any such thing (Eph. 5:27). All the parts should work together in a manner which continually matures and builds up in love (Eph. 4:16). It is a company which demonstrates that it has emerged from the darkness of a sinful world. It is separated unto God's purposes, not man's ambitions. Then it is a true *ekklesia*, a called-out assembly of Christ. It glorifies Him.

**The Dynamic Church
STUDY GUIDE**

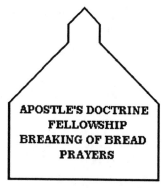

APOSTLE'S DOCTRINE
FELLOWSHIP
BREAKING OF BREAD
PRAYERS

THE PURPOSE OF THE CHURCH   LESSON 2

1. List the three corporate figures of the church mentioned in the notes.

   In your own words, explain how they picture our purpose.

2. Explain one major way that a local church can glorify God *as a group*. (Read 1 Thess. 1 as an example.)

3. What can <u>you</u> do as one believer to help fulfill the Great Commission in your local fellowship? Commit yourself to take one practical step in this direction this week. What do you plan to do?

4. When, or in what way, do you become aware that you are truly worshipping God in a church meeting? Be personal and specific. Give an illustration.

5. What do you expect from the shepherds of your local church in caring for your soul?

6. How are believers *truly* edified in the local church (Eph. 4:11-16)?

7. OPINION: What trends in our own church have the greatest potential to lead us away from our purpose?

8. After reading the notes and completing the study guide, do you have any unanswered questions on this lesson?

The Dynamic Church
NOTES

THE HISTORY OF THE CHURCH   LESSON 3

"And lo, I am with you always, even to the end of the age"
(Matt. 28:20)

The eternal plan of the Lord Jesus for His Church is being worked
out in history. The record is filled with many ups and downs, sometimes
called advances and recessions. The Church will triumph ultimately, but
it has not always been triumphant in its history. The power of evil in the
world, symbolized as the gates of hell (Matt. 16:18), has resisted and
often seduced the Church. True believers, in their lives and gatherings,
have managed to persevere and overcome nevertheless.

The Church is being tested by God as to its faithfulness and fruitfulness. It must face and overcome obstacles by the power of God. If it
were the will of God to have the path made smooth and opposition
crushed in this life, He would have done it that way. Our defeats and
failures are instructive to us. The amazing thing is that the Church has
survived and spread its influence throughout the world despite many
setbacks.

The most difficult part of the Church's witness has been to explain
that much in the world that bears the name Christian is not representative
of Christ. Christendom has often contradicted His character and Word.
The distinction between true believers and nominal believers, between
churches true to Christ and those which are counterfeits, has been almost
impossible for the world to understand.

The Church began on the Jewish feast day of Pentecost (Acts 2). It
was formed by the initial act of the Holy Spirit in baptizing believers into
the Body of Christ (1 Cor. 12:13). Both Jew and Gentile were united for
the first time into one body (Eph. 2:11-16). Christ the cornerstone,
rejected by Israel, became the head of the corner (Matt. 21:42; 1 Pet.
2:7-9). The Church was a mystery unknown throughout Old Testament
times (Eph. 3:3-6), but revealed after the resurrection of Christ. Its initial
history is found in the Acts and the remainder of the New Testament. In
this space we can only briefly summarize broad developments in history,
but these can be classified under certain fairly distinct periods.

1. APOSTOLIC CHURCH (33-100 A.D.)

The dramatic formation of the Church at Jerusalem began with Peter's
evangelistic message when over 3,000 people, entirely Jews, came to bow
the knee to Christ (Acts 2). Thousands more followed. There was a rapid
spread of the Gospel message. The Biblical emphasis changed from the
Law of Moses to the good news about Jesus and the resurrection (Acts
8:4). It was said that Christians were turning the world upside down
(Acts 17:6). The apostles preached first to the Jews, then to the Gentiles

(Rom. 1:16; 2:9). There was an attempt by some to mingle elements of Judaism with the Christian faith, such as requiring circumcision and other ritual observances (Acts 15:1-29; Gal. 2:11--3:12). The idea that there had been a dramatic change from the era of the Law, so that Gentiles were now on a par with Jews, was astonishing even to the Apostle Peter. This necessitated a special revelation (Acts 10:9-16,45-48). Growing resistance by the Jewish community caused the Apostle Paul to turn from concentrating his message on the Jews toward chiefly reaching the Gentiles (Acts 13:42; 18:6).

The Apostles carried the Gospel to remote eastern areas as well as Europe. Tradition tells us that Thomas went to India. The first Christians were out to reach the world for Christ. Paul expressed a fear of grievous wolves, meaning false teachers, entering among the flock (Acts 20:29, Jude). Doctrinal division arose from within. Peter and Paul were executed at Rome between 60-70 A.D. John was exiled to the island of Patmos. It is said that all of the apostles except John died violently. Yet the Church grew, penetrating even into Caesar's household (Phil. 4:22). This initial age corresponds in some ways to the Church of Ephesus in Revelation 2:1-7.

2. PERSECUTED CHURCH (101-312 A.D.)

Believers suffered opposition and persecution during the first century, both from Rome, under Emperor Nero, and from antagonistic Jewish religious leaders, such as Saul of Tarsus. This was only the beginning of a larger scale onslaught of persecutions during the next 200 years. From the time of the Roman Emperor Trajan, at the beginning of the Second Century, to the end of the term of Diocletian in 305 A.D., there were ferocious attacks on Christians with only a few years of intermittent relief. Believers were crucified, thrown to wild beasts, burned alive, tortured and hounded to an unbelievable degree. The martyrdom of Polycarp, a church leader who was a disciple of the Apostle John, took place at Smyrna, now a part of modern Turkey, in about 155. This parallels with the message to the church at Smyrna (Rev. 2:8-11), the suffering church, which also mentions 10 days of tribulation. These days represent the 10 major persecutions, beginning with Nero and Domitian in the First Century, and then including eight more in the next two centuries.

At the same time the church was increasing vigorously, spreading throughout Europe to Britain, and extending through North Africa and other parts of the known world. The verdict of one leader was correct, "The blood of the martyrs is the seed of the church." Satanic efforts to destroy the believers only made them flourish. Another great feature of this period was the coming together of the various books of the New Testament. The four gospels had been collected and were circulating by 150 A.D. The entire body of the New Testament was agreed upon and fixed in place by 170 A.D., except for the final agreement on 2 Peter. Forgeries were rejected by the church. Other books were considered helpful but not inspired. There are no lost books of the Bible. The believers had accepted those books which were confirmed as being inspired, by reason both of their character and their authors, long before any Council made a final pronouncement. A developing trend at this time also was the rise of the idea of ruling bishops in each church. This was taught by Ignatius, an elder at Antioch. All was not ideal however. Clericalism (separation of believers into clergy and laity) grew strongly.

Various heresies about the person of Christ were confronted. A movement called Docetism, which denied the reality of the Lord's incarnation or of God becoming man, was declared a heresy.

3. COMPROMISED CHURCH (313-600 A.D.)

The beginning of this era was dramatic. On the eve of a great battle near Rome, Constantine saw a vision of a cross in the sky, with the words, "In this sign, conquer." His army marked their shields with a monogram of Christ and defeated a powerful opponent. He was convinced that the God of the Christians had given him victory and had confirmed his rule as Emperor of Rome. The State ceased to persecute and began to protect the church. All subsequent emperors, except one, professed, at least nominally, to be Christians. An army of pagans entered the church. Pagan temples were converted to Christian meeting places. Soldiers were baptized as groups. Substantially, the church had married the state, and thus the world.

The church of Pergamos, meaning *much married*, symbolized this period (Rev. 2:12-17). This church had both the doctrine of the Nicolaitans (meaning conquerors of the people, or laity), as well as the influence of Balaam, the hireling prophet (Jude 11; Num. 22,23,24; 31:8). Evidence of any sect of Nicolaitans, supposedly connected with a man named Nicholas, practicing immorality, has been inconclusive.

The now compromised church was joined to the state. The Emperor presided over the first great Council of the church at Nicaea in 325 A.D. The Bishop of Rome was accorded a preeminent place over the leaders of centers like Alexandria, Jerusalem and Antioch. The idea that the Bishop of Rome was supreme over all bishops was developed. It was taught that not only was Peter the first Pope, but that he transferred the power of supreme leader to all subsequent bishops of Rome, and that Rome would remain supreme forever. The division of clergy and laity (clericalism) became standardized. Clergy were now a special priesthood. Other ecclesiastical changes followed: The worship of dead saints (394), the veneration of Mary (431), priests dressing differently from laity (500), the doctrine of purgatory (593), the mass said in Latin in Western countries (600) and prayers said to Mary (600) all were decreed by a church, backed by the power of the state. With all this there was also a decline in spirituality and a departure from the stated patterns of the Bible.

The major outcome of the Council of Nicaea was to stand against the doctrine of Arius that believed the Son of God was a created being, not the eternal God in essence. Succeeding Councils at Constantinople (then capital of the eastern empire and the eastern church), Ephesus and Chalcedon ruled against heresies which affected the doctrine of the Trinity and the divine and human natures of Christ. Augustine (351-431) became a most prominent leader, and his writings continue to influence the church even today. Missionaries went to Russia, China and other remote places, bearing the message of faith. These positive events were outweighed by a tragic turn in the wrong direction. The favored church was less spiritual, less true to God, than the persecuted church.

4. THE PAGANIZED CHURCH (601-1516 A.D.)

To be pagan is to act as the heathen, accompanied by a life of pleasure, materialism, corruption and immorality. During this sad period of church history, Christendom pursued a downward course toward apostasy. The combination of the power of so-called Christian rulers, with the ecclesiastical authority of the Roman Papacy violated the principles of the Bible. For a time, the eastern church, from Mesopotamia to Asia in its Syrian orthodox form, resisted the tide.

This time is called the Middle Ages. During the 10th and 11th Centuries it was called The Dark Ages, because of ignorance, superstition and corruption. It is evident that God permitted the gradual removal of the Christian church in its visible form from the Middle East. The force used was Islam, founded by Mohammed (570-632) with his visions and claim to be God's final prophet. By military conquest, Muslims seized all the Bible lands, Spain, North Africa, the Indian subcontinent, and southeastern Europe, before being stopped at Vienna. It seemed that all of this was divine punishment for the idolatry, empty ceremonialism and disgraceful conduct occurring in the centers of organized Christian power. Constantinople, capital of the eastern empire, fell to Muslims in 1453. The misguided efforts to free the Holy Land by military power, called the Crusades (1096-1244), left only hatred in its wake, along with a miserable moral example by those who wore the cross on their armor.

Efforts to reunite Europe as a Christian political power began under Emperor Charlemagne (767-814). His Kingdom was called the Holy Roman Empire. It was certainly not holy. It was more German than Roman. The official religious centers remained largely corrupt. The Papacy went into a period of decline. Leaders true to Christ stood against the tide and asserted the authority of the Bible in matters of the faith against the authority of the largely apostate church. John Wycliffe in England (1324-1384) translated the Bible into English for his people and criticized the established church for not following its precepts. After he died, official church leaders dug up his bones and burned them. John Huss in Bohemia (1369-1414) preached against the corruption of the church and was burned at the stake. Savonarola in Italy and many others were martyred for standing against the tide. The climax of corruption was the widespread sale of indulgences by the church in order to build St. Peter's church in Rome. These indulgences claimed to give complete remission of all sins in return for money. This so disgusted Martin Luther, an Augustinian Catholic monk, that he protested in writing against his own church. He nailed his criticisms in the form of 95 Theses on the door of the church at Wittenberg, Germany, in 1517. It was the start of the Reformation and the end of the prior era. This period is generally symbolized by the fourth church in Revelation 2:18-29, that of Thyatira. It was a church that tolerated wrong doctrine and immorality, while at the same time maintaining a great display of pomp and religiosity.

5. REFORMATION CHURCH (1517-1700)

The very existence of corrupt conditions in the official church inspired spiritually enlightened men to seek reform. The formal beginning was Luther's protests, but he did not intend it to lead to a split from Rome by many churches in Germany, Switzerland and elsewhere. Henceforth these reformed churches would be called *Protestant* churches, although they, in time, forgot what they were protesting. The movement was an imperfect attempt to return to Biblical Christianity. It was effective in clarifying the message of salvation and the authority of the Bible over church tradition.

There were three basic principles established in this reformation.

26

First, it started with the question, *"What must I do to be saved?"* The answer was that justification before God is by faith in the finished work of Christ, not works of any kind. The second question was, *"What is the final authority in matters of the Christian faith?"* The answer is that it is the Bible alone, God's Word. This authority was not to be shared in combination with tradition or church pronouncements so that the Bible ended up in a secondary position. The third question to be answered was, *"Who will lead God's people?"* There should be no special priesthood that man sets up, with authority over the private conscience of the individual believer, particularly one that bypasses Scripture. Humanly ordained priests are not lords over God's heritage (1 Pet. 5:3). The Reformers saw that the Roman Catholic Church was not acting in accord with the New Testament in most of its doctrine, morals, or leadership.

There were several leading figures in the Reformation. In addition to Luther in Germany (1483-1546), there was Huldreich Zwingli (1484-1531) and John Calvin (1509-1564), who both ministered in Switzerland. They confronted the errors of the Catholic Church with the Word of God. The Reformation did not utterly escape all unbiblical elements in Catholic theology. In varying degrees the Reformers did not see that government involvement in the church was wrong. The problems inherent in all clergy-laity distinction were not fully perceived. Infant baptism was continued and those who opposed it (Anabaptists and others) were persecuted. The idea that salvation was somehow secure by reason of one's infant baptism in a church, even without spiritual evidence in a person's life, was accepted. Religious persecution and killing those opposed to this church's beliefs was continued by some Protestant leaders, just as it had been the practice of the Catholic Church.

The great stirring of the Reformation prodded the Catholic Church into its own reforms. Some of the worst evils of the Papacy were cleaned up. Its reliance on tradition rather than Scripture remained unaltered. At the same time, various state churches became the new religious instrument of the Protestant Reformers. Lutheranism in Germany and Scandinavia, Anglicanism in England, and the state controlled church in Geneva, Switzerland, controlled the lives of the believers. People could think of themselves as Christians because they were baptized into the state church. In time, people adopted the religion of their country as a national or ethnic custom, just as was practiced in the national Orthodox churches in the East.

This form of the Christian church inevitably had within itself the seeds of its own decline. The state churches became lifeless and often remain so today, thus in need of an awakening or revival. One aid for the revival that was to come was the invention by Gutenberg of movable type printing in 1462. The spread of printing presses would make possible a flood of Bibles into the hands of common people in the future. The decline in spiritual life of the Reformation churches is symbolized by the church at Sardis (Rev. 3:1-6). The church had a name that lived, but it became to a large extent dead. Members need to remember the Savior's appeal, "Remember therefore what you have received and heard; and keep it and repent."

6. AWAKENED CHURCH (1701-1900)

Knowledge of correct doctrine (orthodoxy), when separated from the responsibility to practice what we know, tends to spawn spiritual deadness. This happened in Lutheranism in Germany, just as it had occurred in other Protestant churches. In Germany this decline gave rise to what was called *Pietism*, under the initial leadership of Philip Spener (1635-1705). Sincere believers were weary of priestly arrogance, intellectual emphasis, and lack of godly living among both ministers and members of congregations. Pietists emphasized repentance, heart attitudes, personal Bible study and involvement in spiritual work by all believers. This tended to irritate those in the established church who accused them of perfectionism.

Pietism had a powerful influence throughout the 18th Century, one that extended far beyond Germany. Zinzendorf (1700-1760) had a group of devout believers under his ministry for protection from persecution, at a small place called Herrnhut, meaning "The Lord's Watch." Their practice of 24-hour prayer chains day after day lasted for almost 200 years. Their devotion to Christ was exemplary. As they heard about the sad plight of slaves in the West Indies, they began to send missionaries to help. In time, this little group was sending missionaries throughout the world. They were the beginning of the modern missionary revival. Missionary evangelism was Zinzendorf's great goal for the church.

In America, the famed preacher Johnathan Edwards (1703-1758) led an evangelical revival, starting at Northhampton, Massachusetts, in 1734. John Wesley and his brother Charles, together with George Whitefield, led great revivals throughout England and extending to America in the 18th Century. The Wesleys took the gospel out of church buildings and brought it to the open places and industrial areas. Itinerant preachers went everywhere. They demonstrated sacrificial discipleship and stood for social justice. Through their influence slavery was abolished, prison reform instituted, and the poor and needy were assisted.

Independent missionary societies sprang up in the English-speaking world to fill the need which church organizations had omitted. Names now famed in Christian history arose to sacrifice themselves for the conversion of the heathen. William Carey went to India, Adoniram Judson to Burma, Hudson Taylor to China, and David Livingstone to Africa. Their labors were heroic and paved the way for thousands who followed. Churches were planted where none existed before. This evangelical missionary effort was entirely different from the coercive work of the Catholic priests, following Spanish soldiers, among the Indians of Central and South America, Mexico, and the California coast. The evangelicals brought the true gospel, without coercion. Believers multiplied.

Bible societies arose to translate the Scriptures into many languages and to print copies by the hundreds of millions for free distribution. Wherever the Bible was translated and distributed, Christian churches came into being. There was a rediscovery of many precious truths in God's Word. Prominent among them was teaching the expectancy for the Lord's return in the form of the Rapture of believers to meet the Lord in the air (1 Thess. 4:17). The early church looked for the Lord's return at any time. The church of this period had that outlook too. It was a part of their lives and preaching. The joy of gathering in the Lord's Name alone, of observing the Lord's Supper in a simple way with many believers participating, was revived by those who came to be known simply as the Brethren, whose origins began in Plymouth, England, and then reached throughout the world.

This period corresponds well to the sixth Asian church called Philadelphia (brotherly love), mentioned in Revelation 3:7-13, which hears no criticism from her Lord. It had an open door and used it in preaching the gospel. The cry, "I am coming quickly," uttered by the Lord Jesus, was quite real to them.

7. PRESENT CHURCH (1901 TO DATE)

The seed of evil for this period, unfortunately, was planted in the previous century by unbelieving German theologians in the established church. It was academic criticism of the Bible which shook the faith of seminary students and intellectuals first, then the common people, as it spread. It was called Higher Criticism or German rationalism or Modernism. It presumed to be able to question the authorship of most Bible books and declare that they were false. It carped about apparent contradictions. It denied the miraculous. It wondered who in fact was the real historical Jesus, compared with the Jesus taught in the Bible. Everything was redefined while keeping the same terminology. It was deceptive, poisonous, and deadly.

The progress of these ideas steadily penetrated most of the Protestant mainline denominations, until those who were persuaded dominated the official church leadership and seminaries. These churches became known as liberal or modernist, although they professed to be moderate. These liberal churches attacked the groups which were conservative by attaching to them the label "fundamentalist," meaning extremists. Originally **believers** created this term, because they held to Biblical fundamentals. It was actually a conflict between the believers and the skeptical. Confusion was further compounded by new labels such as "neo-orthodox" (which was not orthodox), "neo-evangelical" (which was not entirely evangelical), and "ecumenical," meaning cooperation and consolidation of church organizations under one official umbrella organization. Christ's call for unity among His people was interpreted to necessitate organizational unity among the denominational structures. There was a steady departure of many believers from such liberal-dominated church groups.

There was a massive growth in general church membership until over **one and a half billion** souls claimed to be nominal Christians by the mid 1980's. About 300 million of these were in evangelical groups, but not all of these could be claimed as true followers of the Lord. There was a sharp increase in the number of independent, autonomous assemblies or churches answerable to Christ alone and to the Bible for authority. More decisions for Christ were being made than at any other time in history. Billy Graham became the mass evangelist of the world in meetings attracting hundreds of thousands of people. Radio and television added to this major thrust. At the same time it was true that there was much superficiality of life, corruption, and lack of sincere commitment among these professing masses. Numbers of missionaries on the mission field began to decline. Materialism and affluence gnawed at the vitals of the church.

Starting at the beginning of this century, in Topeka, Kansas, and later in Los Angeles, California, there was the beginning of what has been called the modern tongues movement. This became the Pentecostal-Charismatic movement which has a wide influence. Not only were churches formed to champion these ideas, but there was penetration of these principles into virtually all other churches. There was emphasis on miracles, healings, signs and wonders as the means by which their ministry seemed to be authenticated by God. They divided Christians into two groups, those which were Spirit-filled (meaning those with their doctrines), and those which were not. This caused frequent splits in churches. Many believers of obvious sincerity were a part of this movement. They had a zeal for God, much as was the case with Montanists of the early church period who held many of the same ideas. At the same time, there was evident counterfeit in some claims made when they were exposed to public examination. The group had its greatest appeal to those who were (1) dismayed by the lack of spiritual life in their own churches or (2) had a poor foundation in the knowledge of the Word.

Toward the latter years of this period, it became more evident that the church was in a condition of being lukewarm in its commitment to Christ, infected with a poisonous materialism and proudly self-satisfied. This paralleled the seventh and final church in Revelation 3:14-22, the one at Laodicea. There were still many martyrs for Christ. Believers stood faithful to Christ under intense persecution from Communism in China, the Soviet Union, and elsewhere.

CONCLUSION AND APPLICATION

In these last days, there has been a great burst of effort to reach the millions still without a knowledge of the Lord Jesus and the Gospel. In this sense, the gates of hell have not prevailed against the Church. It has survived despite the errors of fallible leaders and their various groups. Genuine believers are moving steadily toward their destination to rule and reign with Christ forever (Rev. 20:6; 22:5). After the Rapture, the church will celebrate in heaven at the Marriage Supper of the Lamb (Rev. 19:6-9).

The destination of the official, organized church, which might be called Christendom, is another matter. Like Israel of old, it will continue to decline into apostasy (1 Tim. 4:1,2; Matt. 13:33) due to false teaching (2 Pet. 2:1-3). In its combined entirety it is called *Babylon* (confusion), and it will face the judgment of God as it is destroyed (Rev. 17:1-6; 18:1-4). The setting aside of the apostate or false church will be the occasion of the national restoration of Israel (Rom. 11:11-26), just as Israel forfeited its blessings to the Gentiles by its own apostasy 2000 years before. In all of these matters we marvel at the mystery of God's will, as He fulfills His eternal purposes in Christ.

The Dynamic Church
STUDY GUIDE

THE HISTORY OF THE CHURCH   LESSON 3

Read Revelation chapters 2 and 3 along with the lesson notes before answering the following questions.

1. List <u>two</u> outstanding features of the *Apostolic Church* and <u>one</u> dangerous development.

2. Why did the *Persecuted Church* prosper?

3. What was the result of Constantine's political favoritism toward the Church? Are churches helped in any way by governments being involved with their day-to-day workings?

4. List <u>two</u> major trends in the *Paganized Church* that undermined its spirituality.

5. List briefly the <u>three</u> major principles of the *Reformation Church.*

6. List <u>two</u> principles which contributed to the revival of the *Awakened Church.*

7. List <u>two</u> major **negative** trends in the *Present Church* and <u>two</u> **positive** developments.

8. What are some of the dangers which you have seen from looking at church history? How can we avoid these same problems and mistakes in our local church today?

9. OPINION: What most impressed you in this lesson?

THE LORD OF THE CHURCH   LESSON 4

"He put all things in subjection under His feet, and gave Him as head over all things to the church, which is His body, the fullness of Him who fills all in all" (Eph. 1:22,23).

What might be the most comprehensive title of our Lord? He is the blessed and only potentate, the King of Kings and Lord of Lords (1 Tim. 6:15). **Jesus is Lord.** He is the ruler of all things and the King of His people. Therefore, He is Lord of the Church, which is *His* Church.

In the Old Testament, Israel was a theocracy, a God-ruled nation. God was the true King of Israel. He guided and protected them through the wilderness and established them in the land of Canaan. He provided for their every need after saving them out of bondage. Then they turned against Him. They came to Samuel and demanded, "Now appoint a king for us to judge us like all the nations." But the thing displeased Samuel when they said, "Give us a king to judge us." So Samuel prayed to the Lord. And the Lord said to Samuel, "Listen to the voice of the people in regard to all that they say to you, for they have not rejected you, but they have rejected Me from being king over them" (1 Sam. 8:5-7). Though God accepted their arrangement, it was not pleasing in His sight. He saw in the plan a desire to escape from looking to Him daily as their true Leader, the invisible ruler.

CHRIST'S AUTHORITY AS HEAD OF THE CHURCH

It is no less true now, in the Church age, that the Lord is the rightful Head of His people. When someone asks, "Who is the head of your church?," what do you say? We may recall that Ephesians 5:23 declares that Christ is the Head of the Church. Some forget that it is used to instruct married couples that the husband is the head of the wife, according to divine order, and that marriage symbolizes the relationship between the Lord and His people. Is this Headship in name only, or is the passage teaching actual, operational leadership? Is Jesus Head of the Church as a mere figurehead, a title only? Or does it mean something in the practical government of the church?

He is the Head of the Body, the Church (Col. 1:18). This signifies an intimate, living connection between the members of the group and their Leader. **Body** is a group concept, indicative of interdependent function. Life is to be derived from dependency on the Head, just as branches draw life from a vine, as seen in the illustration given by the Lord Jesus in John 15:1-8. In the practical exercise of His Headship over us, He is able to impart spiritual life.

Some would argue that this is a beautiful theory, but how could it

33

work in practice? Is it not difficult to consult an invisible leader? The people around us cannot see Him, nor do we, except by faith. With such reasoning, men have established means by which they often bypass the Head of the Church, just as individuals make decisions without consulting the Lord. Church leaders have set up a visible rulership the same as that demanded of Samuel by Israel. We have earthly organizations with headquarters that actively govern congregations. Often they designate and approve a local church leader. One can have a pastoral head, or a dominating elder, or another leader with little accountability either to the Lord or to others. The church or its leaders can feel quite free to make any decisions that seem expedient at the time, without serious prayer or seeking of the Lord's mind through His Word. There may be little practical significance to the idea that Christ is the Head in such situations.

Some of the doctrinal confusion in the church at Colossae came from not holding fast to the Head (Col. 2:19). They did not see His centrality and the need for dependency on Him.

How will leadership work with Christ as Head? It begins with careful study of, and adherence to, the Word of God. It is the Church's operating manual, not just an inspirational book. It must take seriously the need to present matters to Him for guidance, **through serious prayer, with an open mind**. There must be obedience to every authority instituted among men (1 Pet. 2:13), and subjection unto the higher powers that are ordained of God (Rom. 13:1). Heads of families are human instruments of Christ's Headship (Eph. 5:22; 6:1). Elders of the church are to be honored and obeyed (Heb. 13:17; 1 Thess. 5:13). In every sphere of life there is authority. There is human government, church government, family government, and occupational government. The invisible head is to be consulted in persevering, believing prayer. His word is to be strictly obeyed. Godly leaders are to be heeded, and even unsaved leaders are to be shown respect.

An independent or unteachable spirit among men is a mark of the same attitude toward God. The concept of following some so-called personal leading of the Spirit while disobeying God's provision for exercising His rulership is questionable. We should not obey that which is immoral or illegal or is a violation of conscience. We should be very careful in justifying our disobedience, using the principle that we ought to obey God rather than man. This reasoning should be invoked rarely, and never rashly.

Ultimately headship implies accountability to the Lord first as our highest authority. It means consultation with God followed by obedience to our unseen Head as we rely upon the Scriptures and prayer. Only then can we seek godly counsel from leaders or Christian family heads. We **should not** accept a church leadership structure which effectively bypasses the Headship of Christ, or practices which deny it. Even so, we should be respectful, not defiant or rebellious.

CHRIST'S AUTHORITY AS THE BASIS OF THE CHURCH

"For no man can lay a foundation other than the one which is laid, which is Jesus Christ" (1 Cor. 3:11).

The Lord told a story of two men who built houses, one on a rock and one on sand. It was the wise man who built a house upon a rock which could withstand the storms and endure. It was the foolish man who built upon sand (Matt. 7:24-27). The story was told to illustrate the necessity of not only hearing but obeying Christ. It also stressed the need for proper support for all we do. A foundation is that upon which one builds for fundamental support. The spiritual foundation of the Church, like that of the individual believer, is Christ alone. The poet wrote, "On Christ the solid rock I stand. All other ground is sinking sand." Christ is the only acceptable foundation upon which we can build the house of life (1 Cor. 3:11-15). How we build our house (what we do with our lives as Christians) will be reviewed at the Judgment Seat of Christ (2 Cor. 5:10).

The Church is God's household and is built upon the foundation of the apostles and prophets, Christ Jesus Himself being the **chief cornerstone** (Eph. 2:20). This chief cornerstone of the foundation is plainly Jesus the Messiah according to 1 Peter 2:6-7, which is a quote of Isaiah 28:16. It was a stone which the nation of Israel would stumble over (Isa. 8:14).

The meaning of the Lord's statement to Peter in Matthew's Gospel is often understood in a way which is quite different from this. The Roman Catholic Church sees Peter, not Christ, as the foundation stone of the Church. This church teaches us that Peter was the first Pope (Father), and that he began an unbroken chain of Popes to follow him. Such Popes believe they are exercising the full authority of God on earth in behalf of Christ. Indeed, they call the Pope the *Vicar* (representative) *of Christ*. How could this church come to such a conclusion? In great measure, it does so by tradition. Only one Scripture is used. The Lord Jesus asked His disciples a question, "Who do people say that the Son of Man is?" (Matt. 16:13). It probed their understanding of His identity. Peter confessed, "Thou art the Christ, the Son of the living God." Jesus' answer to him was, "Blessed are you, Simon Barjona, because flesh and blood did not reveal this to you, but my Father who is in Heaven. And I also say to you that you are Peter (*petros*), and upon this rock (*petra*) I will build my Church, and the gates of Hades shall not overpower it" (Matt. 16:17,18). Here our Lord uses what is known as a play upon words, a turn of expression to make a point. **Peter** was a name given by the Lord, meaning a fragment of rock (*petros*). This Greek word is in the **masculine** gender. The Lord then says, **"upon this rock"** (*petra*), meaning a massive boulder. This word is in the **feminine** gender. The rock which the Lord refers to is **Himself as the object of Peter's confession**. This is the one upon which the Church will be built, as the other Scriptures verify. In terms of Greek grammar, the feminine gender *petra* cannot refer back to the masculine gender *petros*, and therefore *does not* indicate that Peter is the rock. The words have different meanings and different genders.

Therefore, Peter is not the foundation of the Church. That honor belongs only to the Lord Jesus. Peter is only one of the twelve apostles whose names are linked with the chief cornerstone (Christ) because of their collective work with Him in the formative days of the Church. Even so, he is only one among the twelve, not the chief. The keys of the kingdom, mentioned in Matthew 16:19, giving the apostles the power to bind and loose offenses against God, are equally available to all who act authoritatively in the church in accordance with God's word (Matt. 18:17,18). The real employment of the keys of the kingdom is in the proclamation of the Gospel, which, when men believe, looses them from their sins. When they refuse, their sins remain with them.

Peter is the most obvious example of a mistaken foundation. People also may place confidence in certain leaders and rest their souls upon the teachings of these men. Millions have depended upon a national, traditional, or ethnic church to get them to heaven through faith in baptism and church membership. They may depend upon some hierarchy of priests, claiming to have received their authority through God. People may depend upon their personal reasoning as the correct guide to supreme truth. However, God's Word, the ultimate authority, says that Christ alone is the foundation of the Church.

CHRIST'S AUTHORITY AS THE LEADER IN THE MIDST

In the Old Testament, God dwelt in the midst of His people in the central place of worship, known as the Tabernacle. Part of His gracious condescension to His redeemed people was to be willing to do this, rather than live only in a remote and invisible world. His presence was signified by a pillar (or column) of cloud by day and a pillar of fire by night (Exod. 13:21,22).

In the New Testament, the Lord Jesus indicates a new order of gathering around the presence of God. He says, "For where two or three have gathered together in My name, there I am in their midst" (Matt. 18:20). Here a **Person** becomes the center, not a holy building. In His post-resurrection ministry Jesus stood in the midst (John 20:19,26). Even on the cross, among transgressors, Jesus was in the midst. In a symbolic description in the book of Revelation, the Lord Jesus stands in the midst of the seven golden lampstands, expressive of the local churches (Rev. 1:13,20). His direct authority over each local church is shown in the seven stars in His right hand, each being associated with a local church (Rev. 1:20). This clearly suggests that each local church is directly responsible to Christ as its head, not to any other person or intermediary.

The gathering of His people around Himself represents a deep desire of the Lord. It also brings to mind His words, "Remember me," when He established the Lord's Supper. He placed the elements of bread and the fruit of the vine before His disciples and called them to ever hold in mind His great sacrifice which made fellowship with God possible. Matthew 18:20 speaks of three things: There is a gathering together of His saints. There is a gathering in His Name. Finally, there is the promise of His presence. These three things show that here is no random company of religious persons. It is the house of God (1 Tim. 3:15). The Lord is there and His people are around Him, just as in the Tabernacle in the wilderness. The *ekklesia*, or *called-out company*, is made up of those called out to fellowship with Him. Thus it becomes the assembly of Christ.

CONCLUSION AND APPLICATION

Since Jesus is Lord of the Church, head of the Church, foundation of the Church, and the center of gathering in the church, He ought to be recognized as such by every gathering of believers. The world of those outside of Christ cannot easily detect those who are the people of God. One reason is the diversity of names. Instead of just being believers (Acts 5:14), disciples (Acts 20:1), saints (1 Cor. 1:2), or Christians (Acts 11:26), we are called by denominational or sectarian names. Instead of meeting around the person of Christ, in sufficiency before God, people often have other church traditions upon which they focus.

The desire of each local church should be to operate as those who are ruled directly by the Lord Jesus. The church should see Him who is invisible; by faith it should be able to turn by prayer and supplication to Him for guidance, just as we do for individual guidance. Leaders should operate under the one true leader, the Chief Shepherd of our souls. The church's accountability must be directly to Christ, not to some central council or governing body. The local church may work together with other churches, but it must be responsible directly to the Lord for its own condition and practices.

The figures of Christ as Head to the body, or Foundation to the living stones, or Bridegroom to the bride, show that a relationship with Christ is the basis of church fellowship. Truly our fellowship is with the Father, and with His Son, Jesus Christ (1 John 1:3). It has been said that each local church ought to be a colony of heaven, a representation of the life of the Lord as its ruler. As Caesar or some other king ruled the colonies of the ancient world, so Christ is to rule His colonies of spiritual life. The colony is made up of those who are a chosen generation, a royal priesthood, a holy nation, His own special people (1 Pet. 2:9). This is not the same as the local branch of some earthly church organization.

The understanding of Christ's headship in all matters of spiritual life can make real the concept that we are more than just co-members of the same religious group. Rather we are fellow-heirs, fellow-members, fellow-partakers with the Lord Himself, as those who have been made alive together. Christ is our life. Christ is our Lord. Christ surely is willing to be the active ruler in our midst, if we look to Him to do this. Then we can become a functioning monarchy rather than a pretended democracy. The Lord desires to be an active, much-consulted leader in our midst, not just a mere titular head.

THE LORD OF THE CHURCH   LESSON 4

1. Read 1 Samuel 8:4-7. Why do you suppose that the Israelites were so eager to have an earthly king in place of a heavenly one?

2. What was the importance or value of God living in the midst of His people in the Tabernacle in the wilderness?

3. How can we express, in a practical way, the truth that Christ is the Head of our local church?

4. Colossians 2:19 describes a group of believers as not holding fast to the Head. What were they failing to do? How, in both attitude and practice, can we look to His headship?

5. What does it mean to be gathered together in Christ's Name (Matt. 18:20)?

6. How can we, as a church, show to others that we are a colony of heaven representing the Lord Jesus here on earth?

7. OPINION: What do you think is the proper thing to do if you believe the elders of your assembly are not operating according to Christ's Headship?

8. Is there anything in this lesson about which you are not clear?

THE SHEPHERDS OF THE CHURCH   LESSON 5

"Shepherd the flock of God among you, exercising oversight, not under compulsion, but voluntarily, according to the will of God; and not for sordid gain, but with eagerness; nor yet as lording it over those allotted to your charge, but proving to be examples to the flock. And when the Chief Shepherd appears, you will receive the unfading crown of glory" (1 Pet. 5:2-4).

The Lord Jesus is the Chief Shepherd of His people (1 Pet. 5:4), not an administrator or executive director. He cares for our souls. He tends, guides, protects, and feeds His flock. His work parallels the work of God in the Old Testament as when David said, "The Lord is my Shepherd" (Psa. 23:1). This Psalm is a remarkable picture of the relationship between the Lord and His people. God is not remote, solitary, and uninvolved in the details of the lives of His people. He lives among them as Friend and Guide. It therefore should be no surprise that those who lead local churches are undershepherds.

In Scripture various names are used for leaders of the church, each reflecting a different perspective of shepherding. They are called **elders** (Acts 20:17; Tit. 1:5), indicating that the man himself is more mature and older in experience in the faith. Elder was a typical name for leaders of tribes or villages in the ancient world. They are called **overseers** (*bishops* in some translations) (1 Tim. 3:1,2; Tit. 1:7; Acts 20:28), indicating the work of those who look after the flock of God. The passages show that both terms are used interchangeably and refer to the same person. The term **pastor** is another translation of the word **shepherd**, used in 1 Peter 5:1,2. This is another way of describing the work of those who oversee the people of God. This is not a hierarchy of leaders, one over another, but a description of the simple pattern which the Lord presents for the caring of His people. It is leadership of the local church by a team of elders or shepherds.

This Biblical description of a shepherd-pastor bears little or no resemblance to the pattern generally seen in Christianity among Roman Catholic, Orthodox, and even Protestant churches. Among most churches there is a division between those called the clergy and those called the laity or common people. Most of the clergy are called by titles like reverend, or even more exalted terms. Some wear special garments to set them apart from the laity. Such men are trained outside of the churches in special institutions. They are given degrees, and even called priests, as though they were a special caste of men. Such an arrangement is not consistent with the teachings of the New Testament. Religious titles were denounced by the Lord (Matt. 23:8-10). If the care and government of the local churches is to be like that in the New Testament, it must be quite different from the forms generally seen today. Let us briefly examine several areas.

PLURALITY OF SHEPHERDS

Scripture presents team leadership rather than a pastor-teacher as the proper form of church government. In Philippians 1:1, a group of elders and deacons are addressed, along with the saints, not a single pastor-teacher. Titus was sent to Crete to appoint elders, not a single pastor (Tit. 1:5). Paul and Barnabas appointed elders in every church they established (Acts 14:23). When Paul went to Ephesus he called together the elders of the church (Acts 20:17). Peter addresses his letter to the elders and called himself one of them (1 Pet. 5:1,2). The concept of a single pastor is absent from the Acts and the Epistles. Attempts to show that Timothy in Ephesus, James in Jerusalem, and the angels of Revelation chapters 2 and 3 were pastor-teachers are not convincing. Timothy was an itinerant missionary, like Paul. James was a mediator, statesman, and prominent leader in Jerusalem. The angels referred to in Revelation chapters 2 and 3 are simply angels, by Scriptural interpretation. None of these are termed pastor-teachers of churches.

Pastors do not seem to have been hired from outside the flock in Biblical times. The system of search committees, job interviews, sample sermons, investigation of candidates from other parts, and financial inducements is one of later development. There was no such thing as assignment of pastors to churches by officials or governing groups. Rather, the shepherds arose from within the flock itself on the basis of willingness to serve and spiritual qualifications. In many churches outside of the western world this is still the way it happens.

A shared leadership certainly is not without its difficulties, nor is the single leader system. Spiritual leaders are necessary, whatever the system, for churches to work well. Form does not guarantee life. Unspiritual or inept leaders will sink any system, Biblically conceived or man imposed.

The challenges of the team leadership system begin with the fact that this is not the way things are handled in most of the Christian world. A familiar habit or custom is hard to break. Greater demands are placed upon several men to study, work, and lead since they cannot simply leave it all to the pastor. They may not know how to assume shepherd duties unless someone trains them. There may be none willing or able to help them develop the needed experience over a period of time. It is so much easier to delegate everything to a paid staff to do all of the important duties, especially teaching and shepherding.

Nevertheless, the advantages of a plural leadership, if spiritual, are significant. Plurality leads to a greater development of spiritual gifts among the men, especially in preaching and pastoral work. Scope is given for all the spiritual gifts to function, rather than expecting most gifts to reside in one person. It gives greater responsibility to the male leaders who function as shepherds when they are no longer termed laity or lay persons. It decreases dependence on one man and focuses attention on Christ as the rightful Leader. In any case, no one man can have all the requisite gifts or bear the strain of carrying the entire load himself. This burden has broken many a solo church leader. In countries where believers must operate as house churches, or underground churches because of persecution, plurality is ideal. The same is true for small rural churches. The joint effort of a team leadership does not require that so many gifts be found in a single man. It permits more than one viewpoint in determining the will of God, and guards against dictatorial rule. The final argument is that the Bible teaches it.

RESPONSIBILITIES OF SHEPHERDS

What are the varied duties of overseers? Unfortunately, among most churches there is very little resemblance to the picture presented in Scripture. In a typical church the elders attend a monthly meeting and review issues that have little or nothing to do with the care of souls. They may head administrative committees which prepare the church budget, or distribute the elements at the communion service. In some cases they are ushers.

The Biblical picture is entirely different. Overseers must be able to teach the Word (1 Tim. 3:2; Tit. 1:9), take real spiritual leadership, and watch over the souls of the flock for whom they are responsible to God (Heb. 13:17). They have the task of genuine pastoral care (1 Pet. 5:2), involving the guidance, correction, and protection of the sheep (1 Pet. 5:3; Acts 20:28). They are the guardians of doctrine in the fellowship (Acts 20:29-31). Failure of shepherds in their duties in Old Testament times brought the Lord's sternest denunciation (Ezek. 34:2-16). God pledged Himself to do what the shepherds failed to do. Certain elders are to be financially supported by the local church, especially if they labor in preaching and teaching (1 Tim. 5:17,18). This implies a full time service to the local assembly.

In summary, we see in Scripture that a team of elders should teach, lead, and shepherd the flock, equipping the saints for the work of the ministry (Eph. 4:12). They should seek the development of the believers to do the various things which are, in today's churches, reserved for the professional and paid staff.

QUALIFICATIONS OF SHEPHERDS

Spiritual or character qualities, rather than personality distinctives, are prominent in the qualifications in 1 Timothy 3:1-7 and Titus 1:6-9. Being an ordained clergyman or graduate of an institution is neither listed nor implied. Being godly is more important than being academically qualified. Spirituality is the most important mark of a godly leader.

The first quality mentioned in 1 Timothy 3:1 is the desire to fulfill the role. Voluntary willingness is mentioned also in 1 Peter 5:2. It is something more than mere human ambition. A desire for a place of prominence ("to be seen of men," as the Lord would say) is a disqualifying trait. Caring for people out of love for Christ is required. The Lord stressed to Peter the care of His sheep as a test of love for Him (John 21:15-17). A man who is reluctant to tend the sheep does not have the right preparation for the job. This is especially true if it is due to worldly interests or unwillingness to bear the burdens associated with pastoral work. It is a different matter if one is simply modest about personal ability. In such a case one should defer to the judgment of others. No man is a fair judge of his own abilities.

There is a difference between qualities important in worldly leadership and those in God's leaders. The Lord made a distinction between the two in rebuking the disciples' ambition to be preeminent as leaders, as the heathen. He said, "...it shall not be so among you." Instead, leaders must take the place of servants. The greatest leader of all, our Lord, exemplified the servant attitude. The corresponding quality of humility is evident in several places. For example, there is warning about the danger of conceit, hence the barring of new converts from the role (1 Tim. 3:6). There is the disqualification of one with a contentious spirit (1 Tim. 3:3); also the self-willed, quick-tempered, and pugnacious man (Tit. 1:7). No Diotrephes (3 John) would arise if this were taken to heart. The shepherd must lead by moral example, not as being one of the lords over God's heritage (1 Pet. 5:3).

The shepherd's role is restricted to a one-woman man (1 Tim 3:2; Tit. 1:6). This is the literal translation from the Greek, and it has occasioned much dispute. Some have thought it means to eliminate the divorced person. Others think it bars bachelors. Certainly it eliminates a polygamist. Clearly no woman could qualify (1 Tim. 2:11,12). The idea of matrimonial fidelity to one woman is central. Effective leadership of wife and children is required (1 Tim. 3:4,5). Otherwise how can a man properly care for the church of God?

In all respects a shepherd must be a man of exceptionally high character, esteemed both within and without the assembly for his testimony. A blameless character is the stated idea. A leader should be a man who can initiate action and make decisions as required. Otherwise he is not a true leader. A passive or fence-sitting man, though otherwise a good Christian, will not make a good leader. He is unable to "rule well" (1 Tim. 5:17).

Any man who can warn, rebuke, prevent factions, promote harmony and maintain good communications with the congregation, is certainly a good leader. Such qualities are also mentioned in the Scriptures. It is important to be a diligent and hard worker (1 Thess. 5:12), even as our Lord demonstrated. Zeal, not laxity, is needed in leaders.

A shepherd must be able to teach (1 Tim. 3:2; Tit. 1:9), especially to maintain sound doctrine in the church. It is *not* said that he must be a **gifted** preacher. He ought to be well grounded in the Word and able to use it effectively in dealing with others. He should be able both to exhort in sound doctrine and to refute those who contradict (Tit. 1:9).

APPOINTMENT OF SHEPHERDS

The assembly is not a democracy, as many think, but a monarchy directly ruled by Christ our King. Shepherds should serve as His local governing representatives. The question then arises, "Who appoints the elders?" Ultimately their appointment should be by the Holy Spirit (Acts 20:28). The congregation should recognize those who both exhibit the qualifications and are doing the work required. A qualified man is not **created** by simple appointment to an office.

Titus appointed elders under Paul's authority (Tit. 1:5). Paul and Barnabas appointed them in every church they established (Acts 14:23). No doubt such men had already passed the test of life and character prescribed. In the present absence of apostles or their delegates, the existing elders, or the missionary who sets up a new local church, would be the appropriate person to make the appointments among qualified men. The people should recognize those who are qualified and active among them (1 Thess. 5:12,13). If there are no existing elders, no missionary, and no church planter, then believers should recognize among themselves the most spiritually qualified people who are already assuming leadership. The elders should be a recognized body, just as with deacons, about whom more will be said later (Acts 6:6; Phil. 1:1). Since deacons were to be tested by prior responsibilities (1 Tim. 3:10), it is also logical to test potential shepherds in this way.

It is not wise to make a hasty decision about appointing an elder

(1 Tim. 5:22). How long do elders serve? No fixed age is indicated in Scripture, nor length of service. It is instructive to remember that our Lord was about age 30 when He began His public service. Under Mosaic law, the age of 30 was required for all who would serve as priests. Obviously a man can no longer serve if prevented by infirmities of any kind including age. Moral failure, family breakdown, absenteeism, and failure to do the job are the typical reasons that elders should step down or be removed. In short, the shepherd serves as long as he is able to function effectively and enjoy congregational support. The wise shepherds will help train younger men as successors and make way for their replacements to become active workers. It is a mistake to cling to any office until death, when one's usefulness has declined or energy has waned.

TRAINING OF SHEPHERDS

Overseers came entirely from within the fellowship in the early assemblies. They were not recruited from outside agencies or from other churches. Elders should know their people and their condition better than an outsider. The logical and most effective method for spiritual development is known as personal discipleship. This was patterned by the Lord Jesus with the Twelve, as well as Paul with the several young men with whom he worked. Discipling involves regular interaction. It includes teaching in the Word, mutual prayer, serving together, and on-the-job training that is carefully supervised. Many leaders have not been trained to do this, but it is possible to learn if they are serious. Materials are available to help. Churches are often willing to share with other churches where they have had successful leadership development, and to seek whatever help is needed to do so. The important thing is to be committed to training prospective leaders.

There is nothing wrong with having younger men go to institutions or training programs that can help them. Many times the needed help is simply not available from qualified men within the fellowship. The point is that the local church should be able to carry out good basic training within, and should not ignore this responsibility. The Lord is indeed the Great Shepherd leader, and the Lord has been pleased to use His key servants to continue to train up future leaders. Elders should guide promising young men through their basic Christian development, particularly in character traits. To broaden and deepen a godly young man in the Word and in ministry experiences is a major opportunity and responsibility of leadership.

ASSISTING THE SHEPHERDS

No group of men which takes care of the flock and ministers the Word can do this well while being weighed down by too many unrelated duties. Elders should not be responsible for the more mundane but necessary matters relating to assembly function. The apostles saw this in establishing the first group of men to handle material needs of the church (Acts 6:2-6). The deacons carry on the responsibility of taking care of the temporal needs of the assembly (Phil. 1:1; 1 Tim. 3:8-13). Other ministry leaders should be trained to assist the elders in the work of the Lord. Their qualifications should also require being high in their level of spirituality. They should be working as "load lifters" for the elders. This training can be good preparation, or testing, for becoming an elder.

RESPONSE TO SHEPHERDS

God tells His people to esteem, heed, and respect their overseers (1 Thess. 5:13). The ideas of freedom and individualism have flourished in recent times. Independently minded and unteachable people bristle at the idea of accountability to anyone less than God. Scripture does not support such attitudes. The word flatly tells believers to obey those who rule over them (Heb. 13:17). The Scripture says that to resist authority is to resist God (Rom. 13:1-5). The Scripture lays down an order of submission to authority (Eph. 5:21--6:9; 1 Cor. 11:3-12). Of course, no one should do anything that is illegal, immoral, or a clear violation of a good conscience. No spiritual leader would require this. Leaders are entitled to protection against unconfirmed or malicious charges (1 Tim. 5:19). They ought to have prayer support from the entire assembly (1 Tim. 2:1,2).

A strong church needs a dynamic leadership, empowered by the Spirit of God. We urgently need God's fullest blessing through godly leaders. We cannot expect to cure a lack of spirituality or initiative by correct form alone. Changes may come slowly and should never be forced on a church in a divisive way. Prayer and patience are necessary. The careful training of young men as spiritual leaders is basic to improvement in shepherding, and eldership.

The Dynamic Church
STUDY GUIDE

THE SHEPHERDS OF THE CHURCH   LESSON 5

1. Read 1 Timothy 3:1-7; Titus 1:5-8; and 1 Peter 5:1-4. List **three** alternate names for senior assembly leaders and indicate the significance of each name. Can you think of any Scripturally unfounded names? Why are they unscriptural?

2. List at least **three** advantages of plural church leadership. List **three** reasons why you think a system involving a single pastor-leader is commonly used instead of this.

3. From the above mentioned passages in 1 Timothy, Titus, and 1 Peter, list **ten** major qualifications for being a godly overseer.

4. How were elders designated in the days of the apostles? (Tit. 1:5; Acts 14:23) How should they be designated today?

5. Being true to the Scriptures, how should the saints respond to their elders? (1 Thess. 5:13; Heb. 13:17; 1 Tim. 5:19; Rom. 13:1,2)

6. OPINION: What in this lesson most impressed you and why?

7. Is there anything in this lesson on which you are not clear?

The Dynamic Church
NOTES

THE PRIESTHOOD OF THE CHURCH LESSON 6

"You also, as living stones, are being built up as a spiritual house for a holy priesthood, to offer up spiritual sacrifices acceptable to God through Jesus Christ" (1 Pet. 2:5) "...you are a royal Priesthood" (1 Pet. 2:9).

The very word *priest* suggests someone who is functioning at the heart of spiritual activity, engaging in rituals or prayers that mediate between God and man. From the most ancient of times, priestly activity has always been evident, both in false religion and in true worship. In the patriarchal period of the Old Testament, the heads of families, such as Abraham, are seen building altars and preparing offerings to God in a priestly way. Melchizedek, King of Salem (the ancient name for Jerusalem) functioned as a priest of the Most High God to whom even Abraham paid tithes (Gen. 14:11-20). He became a figure or type of our Lord Jesus Christ, our Great High Priest (Heb. 7:11-22). Priesthood is a significant and holy office in the sight of God, if conducted according to His precepts.

CALLING OF PRIESTS

In the Bible the word priest comes from the Hebrew word *kohen* which may also be related to an Arabic word meaning "to draw near." This concept of drawing near to God is seen in Exodus 19:22; 28:43 and 30:19,20. From the time of Adam it was necessary for sinful man to draw near to God on the basis of blood sacrifices. Job, a contemporary of Abraham, offered sacrifices to God on behalf of his family (Job 1:5). When the nation of Israel was brought into being by God, His desire for them was that they be a kingdom of priests and a holy nation (Exod. 19:6). Because of their sin and failure to fulfill the purposes of God, they were allowed to have a representative priesthood of one tribe (Levi), selected to serve for the other tribes. Of this select group, the sons of Aaron alone qualified to have one of their number be the high priest and thus enter into the holy of holies, the most sacred inner shrine of the Temple. Even this privilege was limited to once a year, until the time of our Lord Jesus' great sacrifice (Heb. 9:6-14). Now **all** believers can enter the holy place, the very presence of God, by reason of the blood of Jesus (Heb. 10:19-22). Thus, priesthood is no longer a role reserved for the privileged few but accorded to all who have been cleansed through the sacrificial work of our Lord Jesus.

All believers now are counted as both a holy and a royal priesthood (1 Pet. 2:5,9). *This is called the priesthood of all believers.* The Lord Jesus alone is the Great High Priest (Heb. 6:19,20), and believers have been made a kingdom of priests serving God under Him (Rev. 1:6). This astonishing truth was well known to the early church but became obscured over the centuries, until it was rarely known. What obscured it? Obviously the lack of Bible knowledge made it possible to keep believers ignorant. The rise of the system known as **clericalism** in the church created a special class of men who alone were called "priests" and who alone could appoint succeeding "priests." They administered what were known as the sacraments, dispensed the elements at the Communion, stood behind fenced rails at altars and lifted up their hands to bless people on behalf of God. The ordinary believers were called laity, meaning common people, and were reduced to the role of spectators or secondary participants. They had no idea that really all of them were to be a kingdom of priests with equal privileges in the sight of God. Nor did they realize that those who stood in robes before them were merely man-made priests, serving without any authority or status given them from God.

The clergy-laity distinction among Christians is clearly wrong, being based in part on the Old Testament distinction between the priests and all other Israelites. Unfortunately, it is the Old Testament system appearing in Christian clothing.

It may be helpful to make some distinctions between Biblical teaching and modern practice. To understand the meaning of the priesthood today, consider these distinctions:

1. Priests Are Appointed Only by God. "No man takes the honor to himself, but receives it when he is called by God" (Heb. 5:4). In fact, appointment to the priesthood now takes place the instant we are born again, since all believers are royal priests. Old Testament priesthood was a matter of family birth (Num. 3:3), dating back to patriarchal family heads. New Testament priesthood is a matter of new birth, as far as God is concerned. Other earthly priests are simply man-made, without divine sanction, as illustrated in the book of Judges (17:5,6). No man or religious institution has *the* authority to appoint someone a priest.

2. Priests Have No Special Garments. In Israel there was divinely prescribed clothing for the high priest and his associates (Exod. 28:2,40). But that system has been wholly set aside by God (Heb. 7:12,18,19). Just as now we have no Temple, no sacrificial altar, no prescribed rituals or festivals, so we have no robed priests. The attempt to revive portions of this Old Testament system and put it all in Christian clothes is a denial of the present Scriptural order. Someone has called this practice of special priests, special clothing, holy altars, candles and incense "the unauthorized shade of a departed shadow." The Old Testament system was just a shadow, a symbolic pattern pointing to Christ. The Lord has come. The shadows are no longer needed.

3. Priests Are Not Ceremonialists. By this we mean that they do not have some official authority to administer the Lord's Supper, bless the elements, transform them, perform baptism rituals, or offer prescribed prayers before the congregation. Priests have no special powers which are not available to all who believe. Such ideas are in clear contradiction to the New Testament order of the priesthood. Our powers in the Lord are spiritual rather than ceremonial.

PRIVILEGES OF PRIESTS

In a general way a true priest represents man to God and also represents God to man. A priest enters the presence of God, being cleansed by the blood of Jesus. There he prays for himself and for others.

He also communicates with God on behalf of those who have no access, those who are not saved and cleansed by the blood of Christ. What are our privileges as priests?

1. We Have Access to God. Without it we could not be priests. With confidence far greater than ancient priests, the believer can come boldly before God, entering through the veil which is His flesh (Heb. 10:19,20). The Temple veil was torn to permit direct access to God at the very moment of the death of the Lord (Mark 15:37,38). **All** who believe can draw near to God in full assurance (Heb. 10:22).

2. We Offer Sacrifices to God. Anyone who functions as a priest must have something to offer to God (Heb. 8:3). In Old Testament times this involved animal sacrifices, as a picture of the coming blood sacrifice of Messiah. It also involved the first fruits of crops, vineyards, and money. Worship recognized the goodness and blessing of the Lord as the owner of all. The sacrifice of Christ has now ended the need for memorial offerings of animals. We are now privileged to bring other offerings to God in the light of His Son's great sacrifice for us. These include (1) the daily yielding of our bodies to Him as a living sacrifice (Rom. 12:1,2). (2) The sacrifice of our monetary gifts (Phil. 4:16-18; Heb. 13:16) in a systematic way (1 Cor. 16:1,2). (3) The sacrifice of our service (Phil. 2:17). (4) The sacrifice of our gospel witness, which can bear spiritual fruit in souls won to Christ (Rom. 15:16). (5) The sacrifice of praise, our verbal worship to God (Heb. 13:15). Such sacrifices should be offered to God with a deep sense of their significance. These are spiritual sacrifices (1 Pet. 2:5), not petty donations.

3. We Make Intercession to God. From the earliest Biblical accounts, it is evident that men needed others to pray for them (Job 42:8-10). It is stated that God is astonished that believers do not intercede with Him for others when the need is great and opportunity available (Isa. 59:16). If our Lord takes time daily to intercede for us, His people, (Heb. 7:25), how much more should we do the same for all men (1 Tim. 2:1,2). We are invited, as well as commanded, to use the holy privilege of intercession before Him as His priests. Intercessory prayer that is holy is like incense offered before God (Rev. 8:3,4).

4. We Have Satisfaction in God. The Levites of Israel were given no land like the other tribes. The Lord was their inheritance (Deut. 18:1,2). Our great reward for serving Him is the supreme joy of ministering to Him. Another benefit will be treasure in heaven (Matt. 6:20). There may even be rewards in this life (Luke 18:28-30). However, neither material things, nor earthly joys can ever be our *ultimate* satisfaction. **God** must be our complete satisfaction.

Priests may function in assorted other ways. They should be able to counsel from the Word (Mal. 2:7; Heb. 5:12) as the representatives of God. They should be able to distinguish between the holy and the profane, or between the unclean and the clean (Lev. 10:10). They may be called to judge in the difficult areas of personal conflicts (1 Cor. 6:3; Ezek. 44:24). In dealing with the ignorant and misguided, they must learn to be gentle, realizing their own weaknesses (Heb. 5:1,2). All these can be undertaken as a priestly function for God.

HOLINESS OF PRIESTS

The believer-priest today is under no less obligation to be holy in his life and walk than his Old Testament counterpart. Those who serve must be holy and not touch the unclean (Isa. 52:11). There were detailed rules to bar priests with defects from ministry (Lev. 21:16-23). Some were temporary, meaning they could serve once the problem was corrected. Others were permanent. There were many rules regarding defilement (Lev. 21:1-5; 22:1-9). Written on the turban of the high priest were these words, "Holy to the Lord," indicating this high sense of consecration.

This marked emphasis on holiness led many priests to be preoccupied with the ritual forms of defilement. The Lord rebuked this outward preoccupation at the expense of inner purity and consecration (Matt. 23:25,26). Inner defilement is the dangerous kind. It may be masked by a hypocritical emphasis on external matters. Defilement breaks fellowship with God and thus, until cleansed, interrupts the exercise of priestly privileges (Psa. 66:18). True holiness is not reflected in special clothing, special buildings or special days for religious activities. Holiness is a pure heart, righteousness, love, faith, and peace that pleases God (2 Tim. 2:22). It is pure religion that causes a man to visit the fatherless and afflicted (Jas. 1:27). It is a pure conscience that is sensitive to God in things that permanently matter, and thus qualifies a priest for service (1 Tim. 1:5). The Old Testament priest had to be *ceremonially* clean. The New Testament priest must be *spiritually* clean.

The mark of a priest must be that of absolute dedication to God in every area of life. That person is God's man or God's woman. It is separation *unto* God and as well as *from* defilement that constitutes the full concept of holiness or sanctification. The ritual consecration of Aaron and his sons by Moses typified the setting apart of man's whole being for God. Blood was applied to the lobe of the right ear, the thumb of the right hand and the big toe of the right foot (Lev. 8:23). This signified that the hearing, service and walk of a priest was sanctified by blood in order to prepare him to live for God. Our priestly goal today must be the same. Christ saved us to live a life of holiness in pleasing God. Defiling habits, obscene reading or visual matter, corrupt speech, or ungodly associations must be expelled from our lives. Consecration to God of our time, energy, gifts, and other special abilities is proper priestly living.

CONCLUSION AND APPLICATION

It is not enough to just outwardly endorse the priesthood of all believers as a Biblical doctrine in which we believe. It is not enough to strongly condemn clericalism or other practices which hinder the understanding and practice of true priesthood in the church or out of it. It is necessary that we realize the full implications of being a holy member of a kingdom of priests and begin to function actively as such. The truth of God calls for response in an active way.

Since we have access to God, we should approach Him often with clean hands and a pure heart. Since we are called to offer sacrifices, we should do so in all areas enumerated. Since we can intercede for others, then let us not disappoint God by failing to use each opportunity. Since we are to have satisfaction only in God and not in material things, then let us re-evaluate the true riches found only in Christ. Finally, remember we have the highest call to holy living. When these things become true in daily living then we are practicing the priesthood of all believers. Public worship, in a godly way, is an honor for a priest, although not a requirement. However, the private exercise of the priesthood is always available to all believers and should not be neglected.

**The Dynamic Church
STUDY GUIDE**

THE PRIESTHOOD OF THE CHURCH LESSON 6

1. Read Hebrews 9:1-10. Before you studied this topic, what did the idea of priesthood mean to you? To what extent were you aware of the truth of Revelation 1:6?

2. Contrast the attitude about drawing near to God in Hebrews 12:18-21 with Hebrews 10:19,20. What is **your** attitude when you draw near to God?

3. Read Hebrews 10:19-22. What freedom do we now have that the Old Testament priests did not have?

4. Read Hebrews 13:10-16. As priests, what is our "altar" and what are our "sacrifices"?

5. What is the application of Leviticus 8:23 to a New Testament priest?

6. After reading the Lord's words in Mark 7:1-5, what can you do to avoid the Pharisees' hypocrisy of outer correctness, yet inner defilement?

7. Before you studied the New Testament doctrine of priesthood, how were your thoughts different from your perspective now, especially after studying the lesson notes?

8. OPINION: What in this lesson most affected your thinking?

THE DIVINE LIFE OF THE CHURCH LESSON 7

"That the life of Jesus also may be manifested in our body" (2 Cor. 4:10).

The church is a living body of people, completely dependent upon the Lord for all spiritual **life and power**. Christ **is** our life, both individually and collectively (Col. 3:4). When we abide in Him and draw nourishment from Him, we flourish (John 15:1-5). If we look to Him, we can depend upon Him to faithfully provide all that is necessary for our blessing.

God has revealed His character as One who will not practice any partiality. Therefore He is equally willing to bless any company that gathers in His name if they are willing to meet His conditions for blessing. As a general rule, the blessings of God are conditional. Faith, obedience, righteousness, and even perseverance are some of the character conditions which God states are necessary to receive answers to prayer or to have power in living. Jesus said, "If you love me, keep my commandments" (John 14:15). The Bible is filled with stories and precepts that illustrate God's blessing upon the righteous or His judgment upon the disobedient or unbelieving.

It would seem that only a minority of assemblies, like the minority of professing believers, truly enjoy the power of God's life working effectively in them. Since the fault cannot rest with God, the problem must lie with us in not availing ourselves of His promises (appropriation) or not meeting His conditions (faith and obedience). We are surely mistaken if we think that the Lord is satisfied with deficient lives and the dimly burning lampstands that are called local assemblies. His charges to the churches of Asia make this clear (Rev. 2 and 3).

RESOURCES FOR LIFE IN THE BODY

We are inclined to dwell upon the problems and opposition we face rather than the resources available for victory. Believers speak much about the power of the Devil, the wickedness of the world system about us, the general decline prophesied for the last days, and then justify failure. It is also possible to comfort ourselves with thoughts that laxity or decline in our church's vigor are excusable if only we are faithful in observing the correct forms and attending meetings. Does the Lord of the church agree with this?

We need to dwell upon the promises and resources provided by the Head of the church for His Body. He has put the life of God into us personally, and therefore it is present collectively. When that life flows like the nourishment of the vine into the branches, they will be fruitful. God expects fruit. He prunes or removes that which is not fruitful. This applies to the local assembly. God imparts divine life, His seed, to believers (2 Pet. 1:3). The Spirit of God is given as our Helper (John 14:16,26). The Holy Spirit was considered indispensable to the progress of the infant church (Luke 24:49; Acts 1:4,5,8). They were not to move out on their mission until He came to indwell them. Any steps we take will fail without a close relationship to the Spirit of Christ. We must be yielded to Him to fill or control us. The life of Jesus will flow through His church when He is reigning as Lord over His people who are fully yielded to that rule in all areas of their lives. The alternative is to grieve, quench, or otherwise hinder His Spirit. Then the divine life does not flow properly. This results in a weak testimony. In time, the lamp will grow dim or the lampstand will be removed (Rev. 2:5).

Things may seem to be going well with outward signs of prosperity, even though there are great defects within a body. This was true in the time of King Solomon and among other generally good kings of Israel and Judah. Ruinous events followed their reigns. A church may be giving the appearance of life by attracting a large number of people. Another church may excite attention to itself by self-inflating publicity, making brash claims, presenting attractive personalities or musical entertainment which can bring out crowds for a time. Man is exceedingly clever in his ability to counterfeit genuine spiritual life. To such churches, the end justifies whatever means are used. Comparing such assemblies, and their methods, to the Lord and His methods, exposes the former as cheap imitations. The Lord Jesus did not seek publicity, even for His miracles and signs. He would often tell those He healed not to tell anyone what had happened. He never was in the business of raising funds or begging for money. He was not an entertainer and did not use such methodology to reach people.

HINDRANCES TO LIFE IN THE BODY

Some of the things already mentioned constitute a hindrance to **principled growth.** *Materialism*, meaning the preoccupation with things to be acquired or held, hovers over much of the western church like a deadly smog. *Corruption*, even among popular leaders, has made the very word **church** a scandal in the world. Some have given opportunity to the enemies of the Lord to mock both Him and His cause. *Defective consecration* may be the greatest single factor which prevents progress or victory in the lives of believers. This means the lack of whole-hearted commitment to live for Christ in whatever time we may be allowed on earth. *Immaturity* was obviously an underlying cause to the many problems in the church at Corinth, leaving them to be mere babes, called carnal Christians (1 Cor. 3:1-3). Most church pastoral labor is devoted to trying to help the immature or carnal believer, taking time away from the training of more committed saints, or neglecting the task of evangelism. *Selfishness* is at the root of most sinful behavior. The other defects which hinder churches are:

1. Lack of Spiritual Power. The sins mentioned above will certainly block the channel of God's power in any life. Unsensed, unjudged, *unconfessed sin* must be rooted out of any life or body that presumes to ask for God's blessing. God hides His face from us when we sin (Micah 3:4; Isa. 1:15). Godly men fear this. *Unbelief*, or even that halfway place called doubt, prevents the mighty work of God (Matt. 14:29-31). This unbelief may be a factor in our *failure to appropriate* the promises of God. *Complacency* or apathy among God's people has never done anything but hinder His work. In many places the people are not seriously concerned that there is a lack of the power of God among them. They may be aware of it but are not sufficiently concerned to do anything important that might bring about change.

2. Lack of Spiritual Leadership. Whenever God has moved in power, He has used human leaders. He does not need them, because He needs nothing. He simply chooses to use men as His method. It has been said that in the world we seek better methods, but God seeks better or more fully consecrated men. Ezekiel 22:30 records that God sought for a man to stand in the gap that the land should not be destroyed, but, significantly, found none. This implies that God is more willing than we think to seek and use any man who is available to be used. Leadership burdens are great. Involvement is costly. An easier way of living is more attractive. Many are fainthearted or unbelieving. Unless some are willing to stand forth and say, "Here am I, send me," there will be no adequate leadership. Of course, these must be men who love the Lord, not prominence. These must be men who will pay any price, including all that is dear to them to do this (Luke 14:26,27; John 12:25,26). They need not be a Nehemiah or a Paul in ability, but they must walk the same path.

3. Lack of Prevailing Prayer. "Ask and keep on asking," then "seek and keep on seeking," then "knock and keep on knocking" is the force of the Lord's words in Matthew 7:7. Then His answer shall be given, and the door shall be opened. Of course, no believer of limited consecration or faith would often be doing such a thing! This kind of intercession presupposes that the one praying has deep faith and spirituality. Faith and obedience to the will of God are conditions for answered prayer, and certainly necessary if we are to ask according to His will (1 John 5:14). Effective prayer must persevere, according to the teaching of the Lord (Luke 11:5-8; 18:1-7). The greater the challenge, the more needful it is that the one praying will not give up, when he is confident that the answer is within the bounds of God's will. A major offensive in prayer must accompany effective spiritual warfare, and is indispensable to life flowing in the body.

4. Lack of Scriptural Love. When there is dedication to Christ and holiness of life as a result, then certainly it will be accompanied by love to God and to others. God-like love has been called the badge of discipleship (John 13:35). Love can be as superficial as an advertising slogan or a matter of words on the lips. Knowing the great hunger of people for love, it is tempting to talk more about it than to demonstrate it. We can also re-interpret love so that we end up with something other than what is meant in Scripture. Remember that Scriptural love is sacrificial, as demonstrated by the Lord Jesus. It is others directed.

UTILIZING GIFTS FOR LIFE IN THE BODY
How has the Lord provided for the growth and edification of His church? A major provision is that of *spiritual gifts*, which were bestowed on believers after His ascension to heaven. These gifts are spiritual abilities given to believers for the equipping of the saints for the work of the ministry and for the edifying of the body of Christ (Eph. 4:11-13). Spiritual gifts help the believers serve in the assembly and mature in Christ. The Holy Spirit imparts at least one gift to every believer for the

common good (1 Cor. 12:7), according to God's mind, not man's desire (1 Cor. 12:11). The desire for certain spiritual gifts which are mentioned in 1 Corinthians 14:1 has to do with the general desire of the congregation to have certain gifts, especially prophecy, operating within the assembly. Requests for personal reasons do not appear to be in view here.

There is a great diversity of these gifts, just as there are diversities among God's people. Varied gifts are mentioned in Ephesians 4:11, 1 Corinthians 12:28, Romans 12:6-8, and 1 Peter 4:9-11. These gifts have been classified in various ways but such classifications are not inspired by God. However, they are helpful for discussion purposes.

One grouping might be called *speaking gifts*. Examples are *teaching* (Rom. 12:7; Eph. 4:11), *evangelism* and *pastoring* (Eph. 4:11), *prophecy* (which is not limited to foretelling the future)(1 Cor. 12:28; Rom. 12:6), *encouragement* or *exhortation* (Rom. 12:8), and *the word of wisdom* or *knowledge* (1 Cor. 12:8). *Apostleship* would also be in this classification. Another group has been called the *serving gifts*. These include *helps* (1 Cor. 12:28), *giving* (Rom. 12:8), *showing mercy* (Rom. 12:8), *faith* (1 Cor. 12:9), *leadership* (Rom. 12:8), and *discernment* (1 Cor. 12:10). The greater emphasis on speaking gifts has often obscured the importance of the needed serving gifts. The most publicized gifts are called *sign or signifying gifts*. The purpose of these gifts was and is to accredit the presence and power of God through supernatural workings at certain times. These wonders were not normative (regularly functioning), nor were they designed to avoid the necessity of believing God's Word. The sign gifts include *miracles* (1 Cor. 12:29), *direct and immediate healing* through certain individuals (1 Cor. 12:28), and *tongues and their interpretation* (1 Cor. 12:10). The Greek word for this gift is *glossolalia*, meaning a language ability conferred supernaturally without study. This gift was given to speak to unbelievers in their native language (Acts 2:1-11; 1 Cor. 14:21-23; Isa. 28:11,12). God spoke to them in this way because of their own unbelief of His Word when spoken in their own language.

Detailed discussion or controversies related to various issues about the gifts, especially the sign gifts, is a matter for a different writing than this. The purpose of this brief section is simply to say that gifts are given for the proper development of the congregation. They are not limited to speaking gifts, nor only for those we think are talented. Scriptures teach that **all** believers not only have gifts, but that they are to use them, not neglect them (1 Tim. 4:14). Such development requires a great deal of encouragement by the leadership. At least one way is to provide the believers with a listing of ministry opportunities in the assembly and to seek a commitment from each saint to actually function in some way, not to just be a weekly attender. Even the elderly and shut-ins can have a ministry in prayer. It is also important to have teaching on the subject of spiritual gifts, both to clarify misunderstandings and to encourage a response to God's enablements to each believer for service. It is generally agreed among those concerned with the work of the church that unless there is a widespread mobilization of all the saints in the churches to serve the Lord, there will continue to be a lack of workers. This leads to the neglect of important needs.

TEACHING THE WORD FOR LIFE IN THE BODY

The powerful preaching and teaching of the Word of God is indispensable to vitality in an assembly. The growth of the church and the spread of its influence is plainly linked to the Word in Scripture (Acts 6:7; Heb. 4:12) "Preach the word...in season and out of season..." (2 Tim. 4:2). This is the means by which the Spirit of God regenerates, renews, nourishes, and cleanses the souls of men and women. The Bible is well called the sword of the Spirit (Eph. 6:17).

Dynamic church life is regularly associated with strong preaching and systematic teaching. Many groups of saints have been starved through a lack of this. Individual believers will not become strong by listening to sermons or lessons without diligent personal study of the Word. However, studying is often stimulated by a strong teaching ministry at the meetings. One of the things that ought to be taught is the need for a daily personal devotional time with God. Personal discipleship or Bible classes ought to be used to teach people how to study and apply the Word of God to their lives.

Consecutive and systematic teaching of the Word, by those gifted to do this, should be a regular feature of assembly meetings. This should not be simply a weekly evangelistic message or some topical sermonettes strung together on a random basis. Some assemblies have seen the need for at least two hours a week of systematic input from the Word. One hour should be devoted to preaching consecutively and systematically through books of the Bible or major areas of doctrine. Another hour should be devoted to individualized classes which includes the elements of lecture, discussion, and skilled leadership. Such classes should minister to differing levels of maturity. These levels may range from an untaught beginner to a better instructed believer. Homework review, along with class input, discussion and lecture, is important to the success of this method.

CONCLUSION AND APPLICATION

There will be life in the church when there is love for the Lord Jesus and dedication to His purposes among men. There will be life in the church when the believers love the church just as Christ loved the Church, and gave Himself for it (Eph. 5:25). The church should not be seen merely as a place where meetings are held on Sunday, but as a body of people with a corporate mission that goes on seven days a week. Sunday will be seen as the Lord's Day (Rev. 1:10). This verse coincides with early church identification of Sunday as the Lord's Day. It should be as much devoted to God as the sabbath was to the Jew under the Ten Commandments, although in a different way. Sunday participation, however, will not excuse anyone from not serving God the other six days.

The church should be seen as an extension of Christ, just as the body is an extension of the head. It is not some subordinate claim upon our time or a competing demand upon personal or family life. The church should be seen as a collective body in which all the members are the vital and functioning parts. Finally, the church that has a true flow of the life of Jesus will look to the Lord for the full supply of all that is needed to make it a glorious church, not having spot, wrinkle or any such thing (Eph. 5:27). That goal will never be completed in this life, but the assembly should always be moving in that direction, never standing still. Church gatherings should always be an occasion of God's blessing and encouragement to the saints.

The Dynamic Church
STUDY GUIDE

THE DIVINE LIFE OF THE CHURCH   LESSON 7

1. Read Ephesians 4:1-16 several times and consider its meaning for your assembly. What do you need to overcome factionalism in the church (vv. 1-3)?

2. In what ways have some church leaders sought to obtain the **appearance** of a lively church without necessarily drawing upon power from God? Speak from your observations if possible.

3. List the **three** most pressing things that hinder spiritual life in your assembly. How can **you** help to change them?

4. List specifically what you can do to cooperate with the Spirit in bringing revival to your assembly.

5. Review the lists of spiritual gifts in 1 Corinthians 12, Ephesians 4:11, Romans 12:6-8, and 1 Peter 4:9-11. Do you feel that God has bestowed any of these gifts on you? Which ones and why?

6. What are you doing in your church to use your gifts? How and where could you begin to use and develop them? How are your leaders helping you to do this?

7. What are God's goals for us as an assembly? (Eph. 4:13,14)

8. What steps would you suggest that the assembly leadership might take to increase the impact of the preaching and teaching ministry?

9. Do you have any questions or new insights about this topic you would like to share with us?

THE DIVINE ROLES
IN THE CHURCH
LESSON 8

"But I want you to understand that Christ is the head of every man, and the man is the head of a woman, and God is the head of Christ" (1 Cor. 11:3)

Order is evident in all that God does. It is evident in creation's obvious design, and the physical universe with its many laws. God has established an **arrangement of things according to His wise judgment**. That is the meaning of order. The opposite of order is confusion. We are told in a passage relating to church meetings that, "...for God is not a God of confusion..." (1 Cor. 14:33). The exhortation was directed to a church that was disorderly and confused in its function.

Order has nothing to do with equality. It is confusing to mix the two ideas. Order has to do with the assignment of responsibility and the exercise of necessary authority. In the eternal realm, God is the Head because He is **God**. Within the Godhead there is authority and subjection to that authority. The Father is the Head. Both the Son and the Spirit are subject to the Father. Yet there is no inequality. Each is eternally and equally God, a doctrine denied only by cultists and apostates from the Christian faith.

Among human beings, the head of every man is Christ and the head of the woman is the man (1 Cor. 11:3). This is not a matter of inequality or inferiority, but a matter of leadership or headship. Sometimes the phrase "...be subject to one another..." (Eph. 5:21) has been used to support the concept of mutual submission; that is, that everyone should be subject to everyone else. This idea completely ignores the following context of the verse where there is a contradiction to any notion of mutual submission. The verses that follow read, "But as the Church is subject to Christ, so also the wives ought to be to their husbands in everything" (Eph. 5:24). Later in this same Epistle we are told that children should obey their parents and therefore be subject to them (Eph. 6:1). Slaves (or employees) should be subject to their masters (or supervisors)(Eph. 6:5). Again, the order of subordination or submission is clearly stated. Subjection is always necessary toward those in proper authority, including governmental authorities (Rom. 13:1-5). Resistance to this authority is said to be resistance to God. Thereby, one risks His condemnation.

DIVINE ROLES FROM THE BEGINNING

It is interesting to trace the distinctions of the role between male and female back to the garden of Eden. The man was made first (1 Tim. 2:13). The woman was made later to be his helpmeet (Gen. 2:18). The man was to lead and make decisions, while the woman was to follow. In the first temptation, the woman made the fatal decision and the man followed her (Gen. 3:6). The woman was deceived, not the man (1 Tim. 2:14). Instead of obeying God with his mind and will, he followed his emotions and joined her in sin. Satan had cleverly seduced each by having them reverse roles and areas of competence.

The woman's judgment from God was to bear children with pain and to be ruled by her husband. Her desire for satisfaction was to be found in her relationship to him (Gen. 3:16). To both of them, and to their descendants, came the sentence of physical death. The man's judgment was to labor by the sweat of his brow upon a cursed ground (Gen. 3:17-19). Succeeding centuries and generations did not alter these prescribed roles. Christ did not annul or change these roles, as some claim. The husband is to be the leader, protector, and provider. The wife is to bear and nourish children, keep the home and to be a helper to her husband. The physical and emotional makeup of each is well suited for these differing roles. Titus 2:4,5 confirms these roles for this present era. Women have not been slighted, but rather have benefited in a marvelous way by the influence of the Lord Jesus. The Lord Jesus lifted them from abject slavery but He did not change their fundamental role in the family. He did put man under a much heavier responsibility to love their wives as Christ loved the Church (Eph. 5:25). There is no provision for competition between husband and wife, nor for equality of marital roles in what has been called *egalitarian marriage*. Husband and wife are a team but their roles complement each other. They are not the same in function within the family.

DIVINE ROLES IN CHURCH FUNCTION

There is an **order of sexes** within the area of **church** function. This does not deny the equality of women with men *in Christ*, or before God. They are both one in Christ Jesus (Gal. 3:28). Order is not a prescription of inferiority upon women, nor is it an authorization for a domineering tyranny or oppressive leadership. The woman is not to teach or exercise authority over a man (1 Tim. 2:12). The statement is quite clear and unequivocal. The reasons given in verses 13 and 14 should not be subjected to the objection that the rule was only temporary accommodation to culture or prejudice. If we say that the Apostles were simply accommodating the culture of the times when they taught that women should be in a submissive position, we are denying the fact that God inspired the Scripture to say exactly what it says in the New Testament.

Unbelievers often rebel against God's order in society. Worldly, or carnal, believers bring this same spirit of rebellion into the church, wearing an extremely clever camouflage. Scriptural principles that have been settled for centuries have been challenged by ingenious new reinterpretations of certain verses. The purpose has been to make the Scriptures fit modern ideas about the role of women, or democracy, or opportunity. Nothing new has been discovered. Long-accepted principles from God's Word have simply been explained away to accommodate the thinking of modern man.

There are several areas of divine order touching the church. First there is an **order of leadership** in the assembly. The elders or overseers are placed over the flock by the Holy Spirit (Acts 20:28). They are to be **appreciated** as those who have charge over the flock (1 Thess. 5:12), and to be **obeyed** (Heb. 13:17). There is no provision for female elders.

There may be female deacons (1 Tim. 3:8-13; Rom. 16:1), although some disagree. The serious Bible student must come to his own conclusions in this latter subject.

There is an **order of participation** in the public meetings of the church. Preaching and teaching, as well as public prayer at general church meetings is restricted to men under the regulations prescribed in 1 Timothy 2:8-14, 1 Corinthians 11:3-16, and 1 Corinthians 14:34,35. This will be examined in detail later. Women are not to usurp the functions designated by God solely for the men in general public church meetings.

Although this chapter is not devoted to the subject, it should be mentioned that there is also a divine **order of the family**. The husband is the head and the parents are in authority over the children (Eph. 5-6). This also is being challenged in various ways by modernistic movements and certain fields of study (sociology, psychology).

DIVINE ROLES FOR MEN

In the church, as in the home, the man is to be the leader. Only men are to be elders (1 Tim. 3:2), just as the Lord appointed only men to be among the twelve apostles. The feminist movement has penetrated the evangelical world with demands for women to be elders, preachers, and church leaders functioning in the same roles as men. Women pastors, elders, evangelists, and leaders are on the increase. They disregard the Word on this subject or explain it away.

When praying or prophesying a man is to have nothing covering his head. For him to pray with a headcovering is a disgrace (1 Cor. 11:4,7). His uncovered head means that he is to display the image and glory of God. His head represents the uncovered glory and image of God, which is Christ. The woman's covered head and hair represent the covering of man's glory.

Men should assume headship or leadership in their homes. This includes spiritual leadership. Christ's example of love for the church should be imitated by the husband's love for his wife (Eph. 5:25-29). The man should take the lead in prayer at home, and also take the responsibility for teaching the Word to family members. It is a reversal of divine order for a woman to be forced to lead in these areas because of spiritual immaturity on the part of her husband, assuming he is a believer. The father (as well as the mother) is to see that the children are brought up in the nurture and admonition of the Lord (Eph. 6:4). Both parents should share in this. If one is an unbeliever, the other must do the job.

Young or old, women are to be treated with great respect by the men (1 Tim. 5:2,3). The older women are to be treated as mothers, and the younger women as sisters, with great purity. This kind of respect has become a rarity in many societies and many churches.

Men are told to work and support not only themselves but their families (2 Thess. 3:7-12; 1 Tim. 5:8). The western phenomena of the working wife and the husband who studies or does something else while she supports him has no basis in divine order. It undermines the marital roles and often sows the seed of bitter misunderstandings. The working man who sends his wife into the working world to raise or sustain their standard of living is exposing her to temptations, and robbing the children of their mother. Men should bear the burden and keep their families intact.

DIVINE ROLES FOR WOMEN

Tribute must be paid here to the remarkable role played by women in the church. They were prominent from the beginning in the support of our Lord. They were the last at the cross of Jesus and the first at the tomb. In more recent times, they have made up the majority of those on the mission field. This must be said to the shame of men. Women are the backbone of most church working activities, including helps, Sunday School, missionary work, prayer, attendance at meetings and committees. They probably do more evangelizing than the men and are more apt to study their Bibles at home. All of this is something of a commentary upon the weakness of men at home and in the church. There is no reason for men to be less important in the areas mentioned above, except that they have not been taught or exhorted to assume their proper responsibilities. In most cases the women would be delighted to have them do this. Neither the feminist movement nor those pushing egalitarian marriage relationships are likely to improve the effectiveness of men in their roles. Rather they undermine whatever men are now doing to fulfill their responsibilities.

Women can and should evangelize other women by personal witness. They should disciple them, counsel them, do follow-up, form prayer teams or chains, give, show mercy, help teach children's or women's groups, and do many other important things, as indicated before.

Women are commanded to cover their hair when praying or prophesying (1 Cor. 11:5-7). Headcoverings should be worn by women at public meetings of the church. The headcovering is a symbol of the authority of men, and also of the Lord, over her (1 Cor. 11:10). The hair mentioned in 1 Corinthians 11:15 as a covering is not the same thing as the covering that is *upon* her hair, as some have thought. There was no practice in the early churches of women ever going without headcoverings, if one is tempted to argue the point (1 Cor. 11:16). Many still argue this point and have given up the headcovering as culturally outmoded and unnecessary.

The woman's primary role in the home is set forth in 1 Timothy 5:14 and Titus 2:4,5. This should not be construed as a criticism of those women who have had to work outside the home to help support their families or be single parent providers. The pressures upon marriage and family by modern societies has become enormous. Women have proven to be most able in the working, professional, and political worlds. Nevertheless, their primary role is as wives and mothers, if married and able to bear children.

A word should be said about single women. They are relieved from home duties as mentioned above. They are free to serve the Lord, unencumbered by family responsibilities. There are great advantages to singleness, especially in the service of the Lord. Singleness is commended by the Scripture, especially if it enables us to better serve Him. (1 Cor. 7:34,35). In any event, it is far better to be single and to walk with the Lord than to be married to the wrong person, especially an unsaved man or even a carnal believer.

CONCLUSION AND APPLICATION

Much of what has been said in this lesson flows against the popular tide today, even in evangelical circles. Detailed arguments might be made pro and con on various issues. Taken as a whole, without appeals to extra-Biblical authorities or changing customs, the Scriptures cited will support the historic position of the church on this question. It is not traditionalism that is at stake, but Scripture.

Today we have strange ideas about freedom and equality. Freedom in Christ is freedom from the slavery of sin in order to do the will of God, not to seek self-fulfillment. Equality is being equally accepted in Christ by reason of the precious blood of Christ, not equal in roles assigned to others. The Biblical way is not, and never will be, coordinated with the latest thinking of the world. God says, "My ways are not your ways and My thought are not your thoughts." We can be grateful that this is true. The Biblical way is self-denial. The modern way is to assert your desire to please yourself, irrespective of God's will in your life.

Where God has established His order in any realm, it is well to respect it. This is because of the benefits of working within the divine plan as well as the dangers of defying it. The Lord has said, "Heaven and earth shall pass away, but my Word shall not pass away." Let it be so.

The Dynamic Church
STUDY GUIDE

THE DIVINE ROLES IN THE CHURCH

LESSON 8

1. What can you say about the role of women from the creation of Eve (Gen 2:18; 3:16)?

2. How are women to glorify God in the church (1 Tim. 2:9-15)?

3. Read Romans 16:1; Philippians 4:2,3; Acts 9:36-39. Search through these Scriptures for other examples of what women have done to serve God and His people. Give an example from the Bible that inspires you to better service.

4. Compare Galatians 3:28 with Ephesians 5:22; 6:1; 6:5. In what ways are we all equal in Christ? In what ways are our roles as men and women different?

5. What are the duties of men in the church (1 Tim. 2:8; 3:1,2; 5:1,2; 2 Tim. 4:2)?

6. What do we symbolize when men take off their headcoverings in the assembly, while women cover their heads (1 Cor. 11:1-6)?

7. How are the men and women to participate in the ministry of the Word of God in the assembly meetings and at home (1 Cor. 14:29-35)?

8. How would you answer the objection that Biblical teaching about the roles of men and women in the church makes the woman appear to be inferior?

The Dynamic Church
NOTES

THE MEETINGS OF THE CHURCH   LESSON 9

"And He put all things in subjection under His feet, and gave Him as head over all things to the Church, which is His body the fulness of Him who fills all in all" (Eph. 1:22,23)

The gathering of the Lord's people, especially on the Lord's Day, is the focus of church fellowship. Fellowship and ministry certainly should go beyond only one day per week. However, stimulating meetings often determine either progress or failure for the local church. Assembly believers, like family members, must gather together to encourage one another, enjoy one another, and, above all, enjoy the Lord's presence and Word. Most congregations are judged on the basis of whether meetings are lively, profitable, and inspiring. True fellowship is spiritual sharing in the Body of Christ.

If our ideals and maturity were sufficiently high, we would come to worship and serve the Lord, seeking nothing for ourselves except the blessing of His presence. However, only a few have attained to this high spiritual state. Church meetings carry the burden of high expectations. People look for warmth and love, a sense of being as welcome as when they are at home. They are interested in the quality of the message given from the pulpit. The best preachers have always attracted the largest crowds. Further, there is an increasing demand for services which will satisfy diversified needs. Maintaining a **spiritual** focus is a real challenge for today's churches.

The present age has challenged the church with complex problems and stressful pressures. The world's value system too often becomes our standard. Television is a tremendous competitor for the time and attentions of people. Professional sports and other major entertainment attractions make a church meeting seem dull by comparison. The rise in use of drugs and alcoholic beverages creates vast new problems. Rock music seizes and hold the minds of youth, sometimes with destructive impact. In society, immorality and family breakdowns are the rule, not the exception. Yearly more mothers have entered the workplace, often leaving their children to return to empty homes after school. Clearly, the church must change many of its traditional **methods** if these challenges are to be met as we seek to reach the world for Christ in this generation.

MEETINGS OF THE EARLY CHURCH

The first believers had no church buildings and so met together in homes or other existing facilities. As the separation from Judaism became more distinct, they no longer went to the synagogues. The Temple in Jerusalem where the believers met in early years, was destroyed in

70 A.D., and all that was associated with it was swept away. Then a simpler order was established. Believers gathered everywhere to the Person of Jesus rather than to a central sanctuary. God dwelled in people, not in holy buildings. Robed priests, candles, and incense were replaced by believers coming through Jesus Christ in personal access to the Lord (Heb. 6:19).

Acts 20:7 establishes the first day of the week, which was the day that Jesus rose from the dead, as the new day of Christian meeting. The central observance was the Lord's Supper, also called the Breaking of Bread. It was in the aftermath of this meeting that Paul, like others, preached. There was often an *agape* or *love feast* that preceded the communion, in which a common meal was shared (1 Cor. 11:20-22; Jude 12). A second century writing called the Didache, gives this exhortation, "On the Lord's Day, assemble and Break Bread and give thanks, having first confessed your sins, that your sacrifice may be pure."

There was opportunity for many brethren to participate in the meeting. "What is the outcome then, brethren? When you assemble each one has a psalm, has a teaching, has a revelation, has a tongue, has an interpretation. Let all things be done for edification" (1 Cor. 14:26-33). The major church meeting gave many of the men the opportunity to share before the entire assembly and to utilize the spiritual gifts given among them. Slaves and masters met on a common spiritual ground, often in the owner's home (Philemon 1,2). Here was an equal brotherhood, showing respect to those whom it was due (1 Tim. 6:1-2). Most activities seem to have been concentrated in one general meeting, commonly held in the evenings when the work was finished. No doubt there were other meetings for prayer or teaching and sharing, but this was the central meeting of the early church.

MEETINGS OF THE MODERN CHURCH

There are major differences between the simple pattern described above and that which is widespread today. Big buildings with many rooms for various functions are now common. The beauty of the building, its location, interior furnishings, children's rooms and even sports facilities are utilized as attractions to visitors. Well-trained choirs, soloists, instrumentalists, and guest musicians provide a major part of the program. There are separate ministries and meetings for youth, children, seniors, couples, collegiates, singles and other groups. The "center piece" of most modern congregations is the preacher, especially if he is skilled. The major churches of the U.S. are built around a noted minister. His personal popularity is a major key to the church's growth.

Increasingly, churches are dropping Sunday evening services, and sometimes midweek services, placing the emphasis entirely on Sunday morning. Although Sunday School has been a mainstay of the church since its inception in England over 100 years ago, it has been declining in attendance since then. Time allotted for the services has also been lessening. An hour seems to be the limit for most services where preaching is the center rather than worship.

In more conservative assemblies there is a continuation of traditional meeting times and activities. Preaching and teaching of the Word has generally been curtailed. Time for food and refreshments has been increased. Many congregations have grown older by not reaching out to young people, not even retaining the youth that have grown up in church families. Older people are generally satisfied to continue traditional meetings in much the same way as was done 50 years ago, despite the lack of church growth.

MEETINGS OF THE SPIRITUAL CHURCH

We hesitate to use the term *spiritual church* but it is to draw attention to what is desirable in church meetings that will both please the Lord and build up the people of God. A spiritual church is not characterized by dullness and deadness, and should be free from worldliness and superficiality.

1. The Pattern for Good Meetings. Priority emphasis should be upon worship of the Lord, since God seeks this (John 4:23). This collective worship should center around the communion elements at the Lord's Supper, just as the Lord requested of us (Luke 22:19), and the early church practiced (Acts 2:42). Open or participative worship should be made available to the brethren. This worship needs to be warm, overflowing, and spontaneous; not dull, formal, or labored. There should be a separate time for consecutive preaching of the Word of God by someone able to give an edifying and challenging ministry. It need not be the same man every week, but it should be done by gifted teachers and preachers. There ought to be another time set apart for study, discussion, and teaching from God's Word for both adults and youth. The children also need special teaching, care, and supervision in their limited time at the meeting. There should be opportunity for corporate prayer. This may be done at other meetings. It is best to have special times set aside for the saints to pray. Uplifting music, led by spiritual people, should be included in most meetings. Evangelistic meetings should still be conducted in the church building, but real outreach is best done *outside* the assembly. It is difficult to combine all these meetings into one session, even if time is extended.

Small group fellowships or home Bible study and prayer gatherings are meeting the needs of people seeking community and fellowship within the church. Such groups may average 10-15 people in attendance. If led effectively, with ample time for participation, prayer, and sharing, such groups will induce people to come and be involved. Children's meetings, emphasizing crafts, Bible memory work, teaching, and games, are helpful. Women's Bible study groups have developed for those women who are free to attend during the day. There is a danger, however, of scheduling too many meetings, which can seriously disrupt family life.

2. Prescription for Good Meetings. What makes for good meetings in the church? More than anything else it is spiritual people who share their lives with one another. It is also men of God preaching and teaching the Word in power. If both of these components are present, the meetings will be profitable, no matter what the details may be. Therefore, improving the meetings requires raising the level of spiritual life in the assembly.

Some contrasts might be made between good meetings and poor ones. Orderly meetings are more profitable than disorderly ones (1 Cor. 14:33-40). Disorderly, unscriptural, or poorly prepared meetings are unprofitable. There ought to be edifying ministry of the Word and edifying music. We should seek to have inspiring meetings that lift us into the presence of God. A good meeting is when all major elements are well done. This applies to those who give announcements, lead singing or take part in ways other than preaching. It honors God to have things done well. This usually takes preparation and thought, both of which should be the result of the leading of the Spirit. We need the Lord's working in our meetings.

It is important to have those who participate in any area be functioning according to their gift from God. The hand should not seek to do that which only the foot does well. Only the eye can function as an eye, to use the figure of speech employed in 1 Corinthians 12. The proper area of each person's gift usually is determined by the judgment of the leaders, as well as the congregation. A man is not the proper judge for his own gift. The prophets speak, but **the others** judge (1 Cor. 12:20). Some can teach the Word in an edifying way; others are either dull or simply without impact in what they say. Some can lead singing; others cannot. Someone may make a good chairman; another cannot. It is good to channel each believer into the area of ministry for which they are best suited. Some, perhaps many, do not belong at all in the public eye. They can serve the Lord in other ways. If possible do not assign people in church positions for any other reason than when they display divine enabling for that task.

3. Atmosphere of Good Meetings. When visitors or others enter a gathering they sense something in the air. They are warmly welcomed or gently ignored. They sense love and friendliness or coolness. They can also sense joy or dreariness and heaviness. They sense sincerity or a lack of reality in the people around them. They sense excitement about the church, or all seems like a routine. Is there expectancy because God is present to work, or is this only a meeting of human beings not much different from a fraternal club or ladies society? Do they think, "This is a live church" or "This is a dull, dead church"? What can one do to create a good atmosphere? Consider these suggestions:

a. If you are in a position of responsibility, recognize a negative situation and realize that something may need to be done. What vital things are missing? List a few specific things that could be done which might be helpful. It is better to have constructive ideas than negative complaints. Every negative has a corresponding positive. Look for solutions.

b. Rearranging surface things does not change underlying deficiencies. The spiritual factor always underlies the surface problem. If a board has rotted, paint will only be a temporary cover.

c. If you are an attender, come spiritually prepared. Be ready to minister to others, and to reach out to newcomers; to serve rather than to be served. The people themselves determine the general atmosphere of any meeting.

CONCLUSION AND APPLICATION

In the early church there was dynamic power flowing from a constant inflow of changed and rejoicing people, filled with the working of the Spirit of God. People alive to the Spirit will be sharing their faith regularly as a way of life. It is said, "They went everywhere gossiping the gospel" (Acts 8:4). Lively meetings have lively people present. When numbers are being increased by adult converts they bring new life and enthusiasm.

The need for this outreach also tells us that the believers cannot be spending excessive amounts of time going to Christian meetings or activities, which would prevent them from spending time in building bridges with unsaved and unchurched neighbors. Unless there is a determined effort by believers to reach those without Christ, evangelism will never improve in the local church. This takes a great deal of determination and a clear daily priority on the hearts of those in fellowship.

The 20th Century is not the 1st Century, and there have been many changes in the world. The basics of our message have not and cannot be changed. What was central in importance to God remains the same today. Adjustment in details of meetings or adaptations to the culture in which we live may be required, **as long as we do not compromise principles**. It take spiritual discernment to know the difference between fundamental principles and methodological details. The same spiritual discernment ought to tell us when we have very good meetings or poor ones.

The Dynamic Church
STUDY GUIDE

THE MEETINGS OF THE CHURCH   LESSON 9

1. What were the essential ingredients of the meetings of the early church (Acts 2:41,42)? How does this compare with what we are doing today?

2. When did the believers meet together, and for what purposes did they meet (Acts 20:7; 1 Cor. 11:17-34)?

3. Read 1 Corinthians 11:17-34. What things make for a bad meeting? How should a good meeting operate?

4. What is the warning given in Hebrews 10:25? How would you explain to someone the need to take this warning seriously? Why do you have an obligation to participate?

5. What, if anything, might we add or adjust to the New Testament model of the church meetings to make them effective today in our culture? What are the dangers of too much concession to the prevailing culture?

6. Is there anything in the notes of this lesson which is unclear to you? Do you have any unanswered questions regarding this lesson?

THE DISCIPLINE OF THE CHURCH LESSON 10

"Do you not judge those who are within the church?" (1 Cor. 5:12)

The honest answer to this question by most churches today would have to be, "No, we don't." There has been a wholesale decline in clear action by local churches in judging or disciplining the conduct of its members. The temper of the times is against it. Family discipline has also declined. Permissiveness reigns. Society wants tougher measures taken against people it defines as criminals, but it is very tolerant of immorality, drunkenness, lying, and greed, all of which are criminal in the eyes of God.

Scandals have plagued the church among highly visible leaders, to the detriment of the church's testimony. Misconduct and unholy living is prevalent among the members also. In Biblical times these same issues also were a problem. First Corinthians 5 records the Apostle Paul's criticism of the church for failing to discipline an immoral member. He said that a believer should not so much as eat with anyone named a brother who is a fornicator or covetous or an idolater or a reviler or a drunkard or an extortioner (1 Cor. 5:11).

Discipline is not by any means restricted to the idea of public correction or punishment. The essential idea is that of **training in character or practice**, or developing by instruction and counsel, or correcting where necessary. The word *discipline* comes from the same root word as disciple: meaning one who follows and imitates. It has two aspects: (1) Instruction in behavior and (2) action to change unacceptable behavior or to encourage a personal adjustment. One cannot think of raising children properly without discipline. How can one develop skill in music, sports, or even the use of time without it? How then could a church shepherd, train, and lead the people properly without discipline?

The pattern for this is found in God's own example when He tells His children, "My son, do not regard lightly the discipline of the Lord, nor faint when you are reproved by Him. For those whom the Lord loves He disciplines, and He scourges every son whom He receives" (Heb. 12:5,6). God's **discipline** is a mark of His love. He chastens His people for their profit, to bring them to righteous living (Heb. 12:10,11). He has the right and the need to do this. The results of chastening depend upon the response and cooperation of those who receive it.

How does this apply to the church? Some might say, "It may be fine for **God** to discipline, but why does the church have this right?" The answer is that it has the right because God delegates that right to the Church as His representative on earth. The Lord said in Matthew 18:17,18, "Tell it to the church, and if he refuses to listen even to the church, let him be to you as a Gentile and a tax-gatherer. Truly I say unto you, whatever you shall bind on earth shall have been bound in heaven; and whatever you loose on earth shall have been loosed in Heaven." This means that God will recognize Scriptural action by the church as binding in authority in His sight. To be lawfully disciplined by the church is to be disciplined by God. Therefore, any such action is a solemn thing. If the church fails to exercise discipline and neglects holiness in the sight of God, it will forfeit the blessing of God. Read Joshua 7, the story of Achan, in this regard, as well as 1 Corinthians 11:30,31.

DEGREES OF DISCIPLINE IN THE CHURCH

One cannot effectively discipline anyone who is not a member of the community, in this case the assembly. It is not the will of God for any believer to fail to be a part of some local fellowship. If the person is a part of the fellowship, he or she is subject to those regulations which are consistent with the Word of God. This is one reason for keeping the Word in the center of any discussion about misbehavior. The issue should always be what God commands in His Word. This will make it more difficult for people to claim that they ought to obey God rather than man (Acts 5:29), which is a verse often used completely out of context.

The levels of discipline, increasing in severity, are as follows:

1. Discuss (Matt. 18:15-17). Of course we ought to begin in a conciliatory and calm way to discuss issues with anyone. Impulsive and poorly planned encounters, without much prayer, are more likely to produce sparks than understanding. The goal is always to achieve peace and righteousness, not prolonged contention and ill will. That is why this passage prescribes meeting first alone with a person, then with another person taken along, before ever bringing the issue before a larger company.

2. Exhort (Tit. 1:9-11). When people are insubordinate or troublesome they have to be confronted. Deal with them personally using the Word of God. Such people need to be convicted of their wrong doing by the Scriptures.

3. Warn (2 Tim. 2:14; 1 Thess. 5:14; 2 Thess. 3:11,12). This is very close to exhortation. It is intended to curtail problems such as prolonged interpersonal arguments, unruly or disorderly conduct, and even including personal laziness.

4. Rebuke, especially public rebuke (1 Tim. 5:20; Tit. 1:13). If people, even elders, continue in sin without repentance, they must be stopped. Disgraceful conduct cannot be tolerated in the church. If it continues, despite all efforts, then it must be confronted with a public statement. Do not needlessly publicize a matter when a person has fully repented and is cooperating with the elders.

5. Avoid (2 Thess. 3:14; 1 Cor. 5:11; Rom. 16:17; Tit. 3:10). The purpose of shunning is to help another person see that he or she is out of fellowship with God, and therefore out of fellowship with His people. There is a tendency for friends to sympathize with a wrongdoer in order to show love. This certainly is not in agreement with God's attitude in hiding His face from the unrepentant, sinning believer. It is better to show love by firmly isolating someone from the comfort of fellowship than to appear to side with them against those applying the necessary action. The objects of such strict action are people that are presumptuously disobedient, argumentative, troublemakers, and creators of division in the church. Shunning is very close to expulsion.

6. Excommunicate or expel from the church (1 Cor. 5:13). This may have the effect of delivering them over to the dominion of Satan (1 Tim. 1:20; 1 Cor. 5:5). This is the church's most extreme action of discipline. The man or woman who faces excommunication ought to fear. The question of taking this final step should only be decided after exhausting all other remedies, and after much prayer has been made by the elders on behalf of the rebellious believer.

Shepherds must be careful to establish the truth of any charges against a believer. By the mouth of two or three witnesses shall every word be established (2 Cor. 13:1). We must be sure of the facts by either personal observation or verified testimony. Mere suspicion is not enough. We must also be sure that the facts fit the Scripture we use in administering discipline.

MANNER OF DISCIPLINE IN THE CHURCH

How we administer discipline is just as important as the discipline itself. Harsh, impulsive, abrupt actions or words can wound. If discipline is done rightly, there is less cause for criticism. It may not always be justified in view of the facts, but it is still sad to hear the words, "It was not done in love." It has been said that the *goal* of all discipline, including that of God, is **restoration**. Indeed, He has been called the God of recovery. That has been a source of comfort to millions. If this is our object too, then we ought to act in a manner best suited to produce recovery.

Galatians 6:1 sets the tone for this section, in which it is stated, "Brethren, if a man is caught in any trespass, you who are spiritual, restore such a one in a spirit of gentleness; each one looking to yourself lest you too be tempted." We note that there is a requirement of spirituality needed for the work of restoring an erring brother. Discipline with the spirit of gentleness or meekness in the approach. We must remember that but for the grace of God there might I be. Any discipline will be more acceptable if given with this humbling thought.

Partiality or unfairness, which treats people with the same problem in a different way, is not acceptable. Even children are extremely sensitive to unfairness. The Lord Jesus was thoroughly impartial in all his dealings. Whether rich or poor, influential or not, *all* people should be treated in an equitable way. James 2:1,9 applies this principle to someone fawning over a wealthy person who may come to the assembly. No partiality is acceptable in disciplinary matters. The families of the prominent should be treated no differently from other church families when discipline is administered.

Patience, firmness, steadfastness, and a constructive approach are important in dealing with misbehavior. This does not imply weakness. One must remember both the goodness and the severity of God (Rom. 11:22). To confront, rebuke, and even expel is tough action. That is why it is avoided by most leaders. They would prefer to allow errors, and leave it to the Lord to discipline others. The great phrase, "speaking the **truth** in love" (Eph. 4:15) conveys the two things necessary. Being gentle, patient, and not quarrelsome is commended (2 Tim. 2:24).

Forbearance and forgiveness is set forth in Colossians 3:13. If this is our manner, the results will more likely be favorable. Such attitudes melt, rather than harden the hearts of offenders.

SUBJECTS OF DISCIPLINE IN THE CHURCH

Everyone in the church must remember that we are all subject to the discipline and training of God. We are part of a family, not individualists. Because we are, or ought to be, a close-knit family, we must care enough about each other to correct the kind of behavior that is harmful. When people are in need, some believers seem to have little trouble in asking for help. When they behave in a questionable way, they are more likely to reject efforts to correct their path. The wise and discerning leader seeks out those who stray. The shepherds must seek the wandering sheep ... if they truly care about the flock.

Who should be a part of this local fellowship that is under both the Great Shepherd and His undershepherds? In the general world of Christianity, virtually any vague profession of faith in Jesus is accepted as adequate. Often people are admitted without having to give a clear testimony of their salvation. The desire for members, and therefore contributors, is so great that a mere desire to join the church is accepted. A higher standard would be to make sure that only those people who belong to Christ will be a part of the local assembly. The church can only properly discipline those who are explicitly in fellowship. Therefore, discipline in the church begins by determining who is committed to the Lord, the church, and its leadership.

The Biblical requirement is to receive all whom Christ has received (Rom. 15:7). How can we know whom Christ has received? Do they confess with their mouth that Jesus is Lord and believe in their hearts that God raised Him from the dead (Rom. 10:9)? Do they appear to be His true followers, not just people mouthing certain familiar words? Not everyone who says "Lord, Lord" will enter the Kingdom (Matt. 7:21). Have they obeyed the Lord in believer's baptism, as He commanded (Matt. 28:19)? Remember that the section in 1 John 3:4-10 ends with this statement, "By this the children of God and the children of the devil are obvious: any one who does not practice righteousness is not of God, nor the one who does not love his brother." A person's life should make this obvious. Then we ought to be able to discern who is a believer and who is not.

Elements of essential doctrine that true believers have historically held, whatever their religious affiliation, should be accepted by those in fellowship. These doctrines include the Deity of Christ, the Trinity, the inspiration and authority of the Word of God, the reality of heaven and hell, and salvation by grace without works, through the finished work of the Lord Jesus on the Cross.

What else should be expected? True fellowship with God depends on walking in the light. If we walk in the light as He is in the light we have fellowship with one another, and the blood of Jesus Christ His Son cleanses us from all sin (1 John 1:7). Fellowship with other believers is also conditional on walk. When a person is under the discipline of God or when he does not walk in the truth or the light, he should not be received into fellowship until the matter is resolved. We ought to assist in restoring a wayward believer as much as we can. However, allowing shallow repentance or a light handling of serious questions invites sinful repetition in the future.

CONCLUSION AND APPLICATION

Discipline carried out in a godly manner by a local church has a refining or purifying effect. When we grieve the Holy Spirit by neglecting discipline, we hinder open lines of communication with God. The Lord of the Church should not need to come to the assembly and call for repentance as He does in Revelation chapters 2 and 3. The Lord calls us to a high standard of holiness by holding us accountable for lives that will not be a discredit to Him or His Church. Discipline benefits the saints individually, who are the subjects of disciplinary action, by bringing them back to a walk that pleases God.

The Judgment Seat of Christ is the ultimate place of accountability for life and service for all believers (2 Cor. 5:10; 1 Cor. 3:12-15). Even though our sins have been paid for and washed away in the blood of Christ, it does not mean that we can avoid having our life and service evaluated. Judgment begins at the house of God, we are told in 1 Peter 4:17. God denounced the spiritual leaders in both the Old and New Testaments for being lax in the exercise of discipline among His people. He repeatedly judged the unfaithfulness and sin of even ordinary people who professed faith in Him. If we are to be a healthy body of believers it is critical that we exercise discipline in the church.

The Dynamic Church
STUDY GUIDE

THE DISCIPLINE OF THE CHURCH   LESSON 10

1. Define **discipline** (as you understand it from the lesson notes) as it applies to the church.

2. What happened in the church in Corinth, according to 1 Corinthians 5, that caused Paul's rebuke?

3. What is God's motivation and goal in disciplining His children (Heb. 12:6,10)?

4. Who **should** be received into fellowship (Rom. 15:7; 14:1)?

5. Who **should not** be received into fellowship (2 John 9,10; Gal. 5:19-21)? When should we refuse to fellowship with another believer (1 Cor. 5:11; Rom. 16:17; Tit. 3:10,11)?

6. How can the church avoid chastening from God or the withholding of His blessings (1 Cor. 11:31; 5:12,13; Rev. 2:5,14-16; 3:15,16,19)?

7. What do you learn from the story of Achan in Joshua chapter 7?

8. Various degrees of discipline are indicated in the verses below. Complete the chart under the two headings.

TO TAKE	OFFENSE	ACTION
a. 1 Thess. 5:14a		
b. 2 Thess. 3:10-14		
c. 1 Tim. 5:20		
d. 1 Cor. 5:11,13		

9. OPINION: Can you remember any church disciplinary action of which you were personally aware? What was your reaction to it?

10. Do you have any unanswered questions on this lesson?

EVANGELISM AND THE CHURCH   LESSON 11

"And the Lord was adding to their number day by day those who were being saved" (Acts 2:47).

The central purpose of the Lord Jesus was to reach the lost. That is why He came to earth (Luke 19:10). He explained His association with sinners in the triple parables of the lost sheep, the lost coin, and the lost son (Luke 15) to show that His mission was to save sinners. In His initial call to the first followers He invited them to come so that He might make them fishers of men (Mark 1:17). His last message prior to His ascension reminded them that they were to be His witnesses in the world. The first post-Pentecostal message was evangelistic (Acts 2:37-38). The first believers evangelized constantly (Acts 5:42; 8:4). If any group of believers desires to function as a New Testament church then it must be an evangelizing church. There would have been no spread of the Gospel in the world at the time without such an effort. There will be no spread of the message now without the people of God doing the same.

It is mandatory for the spiritual health of any assembly not only to believe the gospel, but also to effectively spread the gospel. This means that it must have a strong outreach effort that adds souls to the church. It has been well said, "Evangelize or die." God seems to be with those assemblies in a special way who have the burden for the lost and do something about it. Transfer growth (people coming from other churches) and biological growth (numerical increase by the birth of children to the families of believers) is not true spiritual growth in the sense of reaching those who have not clearly heard and responded to the Gospel. We are not simply called to *hold the fort* (stay within our walls defensively) but to *attack* the fort, (meaning the **gates of hell**) where there are barriers to the truth. Evangelism is rightly called outreach.

It has been argued that only the Spirit of God regenerates the spiritually dead and that the responsibility rests upon Him to make any necessary moves. This fails to recognize that believers have been given the ministry of reconciliation (2 Cor. 5:18,20) and we are ambassadors for Christ. Not every one has the gift of an evangelist, but every believer has the responsibility to share the message of life by example and by word to those within his own circle of witness. Human agency in the salvation of others is indicated by Paul's claim to have begotten some to salvation through the Gospel, and therefore to be their spiritual father (1 Cor. 4:15; Philemon 10). Those who come to God through our ministry will be our eternal joy, crown and glory (1 Thess. 2:19). He that winneth souls is wise (Prov. 11:30). He who turns a sinner from the error of his way will save his soul from death and will cover a multitude of sins (Jas. 5:20). God has chosen to use us as His witnesses.

Unless we seek to remove all things that are obstacles to our obedience to God in this matter, there will not likely be continuing evangelistic fruit. Some general things are quite difficult to change. Deficient leadership is a problem in any area of church life. Both prayer and spiritual initiative are important. Aging congregations often lack the energy to reach out. Some assemblies are located in areas of population in which there is a very different culture or ethnic background from the congregation. Most of the believers may live many miles from the meeting place. This makes it difficult to reach the local community for Christ.

There are other factors which hinder the fervent evangelism in an assembly.

1. Lack of Spiritual Vitality. Effective witnessing is really an overflow of spiritual life, resulting from the filling of the Spirit and energy from God. When believers are complacent, lazy, prayerless, and living at a low level of commitment to Christ, there will be little soul-winning. Affluence and materialism are major contributors to this weakness.

2. Fear of Man. Many believers fail to share their faith within their nearest circle of regular contacts because they are afraid of rejection, ridicule or offending someone. The fear of man is not of God (2 Tim 1:7) but brings a snare (Prov. 29:25). Some training, encouragement, and a little practice in low key situations, can offset this lack of self-confidence.

3. Lack of Purpose to Reach Out. Unless, through prayer and teaching from the Word, both the church elders and those in fellowship make up their minds to obey the Lord and share His concern for the lost, things will continue as before. Commitments must be made, goals set, methods reviewed, and prayer intensified to achieve this end. We must be striving together for the faith of the gospel (Phil. 1:27).

4. Not Being Open to New People. Many believers make no effort to invite unchurched people into their homes or to build bridges of friendship to the unsaved. They keep their doors open only for other believers. At the assembly meetings, there is sometimes a lack of warmth and friendly receptivity to visitors. New people often bring their problems, and even strange behavior, into the meetings. You may avoid embarrassing problems by not bringing in elements that disturb us. Therefore we may be tempted to act coolly towards those who are not like us. We then become a closed, religious club, not an evangelizing church.

5. Inflexibility in Methods. It cannot be said that the New Testament prescribes a strict way of reaching the unsaved. Only the message remains unchangeable. In former times, tent meetings, week long gospel meetings, and street preaching have been effective in reaching many with the message of salvation. In some places these methods are still profitable, however we need to be alert to new approaches People are not as readily disposed to visit a church on the corner, or to attend Sunday evening, or go to special evangelistic meetings. We have the competition of television, sports spectaculars, and over-abundant recreation made possible by increased living standards. If we do not upgrade our methods of making contacts, we will soon have few new converts. We should be seeking interested people by person-to-person conversation and effort.

6. Lack of Leaders Who Model Evangelistic Outreach. The drive to reach out to the lost is usually led by one or more people in the meetings. They generate the effort, the enthusiasm, and the conscience-prodding that gets things going. They show others how, and win souls themselves. This is a great stimulus. If such a person is not available, then prayer should be made for concerned individuals to meet together and then seek someone to take the lead.

7. Not Accepting Personal or Church Responsibility. We can't evade our responsibility for our failure to win souls by pointing to our token efforts. We can say that we have certain gospel meetings, or evangelistic speakers, or the Sunday School, or the summer camp effort. We can contribute to programs that do evangelism. The point is that when we ourselves don't do it the church sees little fruit in this ministry. This remains a serious problem before God. We need to face the issue and do something to change things.

MAKING INSIDE IMPROVEMENTS FOR EVANGELISM
It may be necessary to set our own houses in order, especially at church gatherings, before trying to bring in unsaved visitors. If we cannot retain visitors after their first or second time in coming, then we are wasting opportunities. Often visitors have no desire to come back. Why is this?

1. Are they **warmly greeted** at the door, made to feel at home, and introduced to some of the believers? Did you politely obtain their names and addresses (guest register or visitor cards) with a view to encouraging further contact and communication?

2. **Hospitality**, meaning an invitation to dinner that day or in the future, is used by many churches. There may even be a dinner served at the church itself to which they are invited. A follow-up phone call can also convey the message of welcome.

3. The **quality of the meeting** itself is affected by several factors. Was the song-leading well done, the special musical numbers of good quality, the chairman's job pleasantly performed? Did we keep out the "in-house" talk, jargon and first name references that others don't recognize? Were announcements kept to a minimum so that they are not boring? Visitors notice these things.

4. How good was the **preaching**? Was it a strong, expository message done in a lively, interesting and spiritual manner by someone with evident gift? This is the kind that brings them back. It also encourages people to invite their friends.

5. If they should be won to Christ, will there be **prompt follow up** help for the new believer? This should be done by the appropriate person, who has training or preparation. This work conserves the fruit of evangelism.

6. If visitors should keep coming and want to become a part of fellowship, either by conversion or transfer, what will be done to involve them in the life of the assembly? **Involvement** helps us both to retain and help people to minister according to their gifts and talents.

7. Do you have **special classes** and groups to attract those with certain interests? How good is your youth group and its leadership, whether high school, college or others? Do you have electives for adult Bible Study? Is there any provision for a singles ministry, a couple's

class, or for such handicapped groups as the deaf (requiring an interpreter)? It is said that churches which keep starting new groups are the ones which attract the most visitors.

8. Do you have reserved parking for visitors and a reserved section of <u>good</u> seats for visitors who may come late? How are the nursery and preschool facilities and services?

9. Is there regular special **prayer** for evangelistic fruit? Do you have any goals in this area? Is there any planning about how to increase visitors coming to services? What plans and strategies have been laid out by the elders and other leaders of the church to reach your community for Jesus Christ?

MAKING OUTSIDE CONTACTS FOR EVANGELISM

Assemblies that are effective in evangelism have learned to move much of the effort outside the walls of the church in order to penetrate into the community. The vast majority of people that need to be reached probably will not get dressed to come to a church meeting in order to hear the Gospel. The message of the New Testament is to **go**, not to invite people to come and **visit us**.

Any such plan must begin by creating an evangelism consciousness in the assembly so that believers have a burden to share their faith. Probably no more than 10% of the saints will get over their unwillingness to begin sharing with those in their own daily circle. However, even this percentage will not be realized without a strong stimulus. Those being saved come from a web or network of contacts around the believers, such as relatives, friends and neighbors. This is especially true of those around new believers who are often active in witnessing during their first year or two after conversion. There must be some strategy for making sure this happens to the maximum possible extent. About 90% of our best prospects will come from these new networks.

There is really no one best avenue of evangelistic prospects. The more strategies that are followed, the more prospects will be contacted. It is good to be aware that those who have a sense of need, or have a crisis, are most open to consider spiritual things. Those who are seriously ill may be open to a call. This is true for a person who has just had a marriage break-up. Someone may have a teenager or child about whom he or she is concerned. Human needs can be open doors.

Consider some of the following possibilities:

1. Do some **direct mailing** to the neighborhood, particularly to those moving into the community. Attractive pieces, sent repeatedly, will yield some contacts if you continue for a while. One-shot mailings are generally not effective. Keeping a list of visitors and neighborhood contacts can be helpful.

2. Establish informal **home gatherings** (small groups or cells) and gradually begin to include neighbors. These will most likely come when you have made an effort to build bridges to them by informal, non-religious conversation, and by being helpful. Do a low-key study of a book like John's Gospel, or have a group to discuss how to strengthen marriages. There are some videos with Christian messages or programs now available for those who have VCR's. At first, people may be more likely to visit your home than to come to your church.

3. Families may have a concern for their kids or teenagers when they have no spiritual concern themselves. A **program of crafts, games, activities, and Bible memory work** may be popular with children from ages 5-12. These are usually done one evening a week.

4. **Youth activities**, directed by committed leaders, are an important part of attracting new people at an age when they are most open to spiritual things.

5. Special programs can be set up for those who have problems with drugs or alcohol. These are best run by converts who have been delivered from these habits.

6. You can add singles ministries, seniors activities, ladies Bible studies, day care centers. Many churches have even established private schools, although this can impose a great demand on your people, finances, and focus.

Train a core of committed people in home visitation so that when you have new contacts you can have the teams call on them. These people, men and women, can be trained to either present the Gospel in a systematic way, or give pastoral care. These trainees should progress to the point where they can train others. All team members should be taught to share Christ regularly with their own circle of contacts. For an effective evangelistic team, select people to whom Christ is truly Lord and through whom His life is shown. When we demonstrate care for people and reach out to them, they are attracted to Christ.

Those who witness have a strong conviction that people are doomed without Christ (John 3:18; 8:24). They have learned to give their testimony simply and powerfully. They believe God will use them to win souls to Christ, and they are seeking to do it. For such people God arranges special appointments with needy souls (John 4:4-15).

Effective soul-winners are not just reaching for *decisions*, a term which may have outlived its usefulness. They are seeking to win people to a sincere commitment to follow Christ in this life. They do a thorough, careful work without hurrying people into false professions. True conversions must include a basic knowledge of the gospel, genuine repentance, and yieldedness to Christ.

CONCLUSION AND APPLICATION

Evangelism in the church is not just a program or a meeting from time to time. It is a burden felt deeply by a body of people concerning the eternal destiny of the multitudes around them facing a Christless eternity. Evangelism comes from a powerful sense of responsibility for the lost. When we accept Jesus' purpose for His own life--to seek and save the lost--as our purpose, we begin to evangelize. The church must take this commission seriously and work at it. Where necessary, it must consider more creative and varied ways of outreach.

Any assembly which determines that it will be available to the Holy Spirit for outreach in winning souls to Christ will be blessed by God. The **will** to do it must precede the decision on the **way** it is to be done. May we be moved to this task with urgency!

The Dynamic Church
STUDY GUIDE

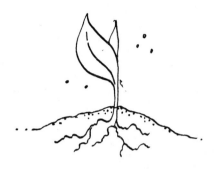

EVANGELISM AND THE CHURCH   LESSON 11

1. Read Acts 2:47. What was happening in the early church?

2. From Acts 6:7, what can you learn about the qualities of the new converts in the church?

3. Among the various hindrances to effective evangelism, list the <u>two</u> that most impress you. What needs to be done to overcome them?

4. Philippians 1:27 is a four-part instruction to a church. What elements of this instruction are we as a church doing well in? Where are we failing?

5. Read Titus 3:1-9. What are the attractions, attitudes, and message of a good witness?

6. How do you make contacts with unsaved people to whom you witness? Can you relate any positive experiences which you have had through your efforts?

7. What are the effects of a holy church upon unbelievers (Acts 5:12-14; 1 Cor. 14:23,24)?

8. OPINION: How can evangelistic effectiveness be improved concerning the congregation's individual witness **outside** the church?

9. Is there anything in this lesson which you do not understand?

**The Dynamic Church
NOTES**

THE DISCIPLING OF THE CHURCH LESSON 12

"Go therefore and make disciples of all the nations, baptizing them in the name of the Father and the Son and the Holy Spirit, teaching them to observe all that I commanded you" (Matt. 28:19-20).

If the whole world repented of sins, believed in the Lord Jesus, was baptized and even added to the church, but then stopped with this, the full commission of Christ would still be unmet. How could such a statement be made? Because we would have halted short of the Lord's command to make them all into His disciples, and teach them to observe or obey all that He commanded.

The faithful proclamation of the Gospel message is only the beginning of a process. Professions or decisions for Christ are not the final goal. Even when baptized and added to the church, converts often remain spectators rather than ministers of Christ. This leaves believers in a state of infancy or retarded development. The fact that so many churches have been described as a sea of mediocrity and carnality as to spiritual life is because of lack of development. This was the condition of the Corinthians (1 Cor 3:1-3) as well as some among the Jewish converts (Heb. 5:12-14). Often believers have heard clear challenges to live a life of victory and fruitfulness but have neglected to respond. They lag behind in their path to a higher calling in life and neglect to grow. Their numbers are great enough so that they dictate the spiritual tone and lifestyle of those churches. Their lives do not conform to the will of the Lord. They may persecute or criticize those who seek to arouse them to greater progress.

The Apostle Paul caught the true vision of God's purpose for us to admonish every man and teach every man, with all wisdom, that we may present every man complete in Christ (Col. 1:28). The most common invitation of the Lord Jesus to His audience was "Follow Me." It was a life to be lived on earth, not a ticket to Heaven. It is God's will that His people be part of a congregation of obedient disciples or true followers. Discipling is an activity to be carried on within the local church.

If it is God's will for the church to devote its energies to making genuine disciples, then what is the plan to achieve this? What is the degree of the commitment of the leaders to this idea? Are any of the leaders willing to be personally involved? These questions deserve consideration.

WHAT IS A DISCIPLE?

The meaning of the word disciple is learner. In practical usage it had the clear idea of one who followed a certain teacher. Such learners listened, imitated and obeyed their chosen leader. They helped spread his teachings. No person would be considered a disciple who only mentally agreed with some of his teacher's ideas, but failed to practice them.

The word was not unique to the followers of Jesus. There were those who claimed to be Moses' disciples (John 9:28) or John the Baptist's disciples (Matt. 9:14). The fact that they made the claim did not mean that it was true. With reference to Christ, disciple was another word for those who believed in Him (Acts 6:1-2). However, the Lord noted those who were **disciples indeed**, or true disciples (John 8:31). This meant that they lived up to their name. The Scripture tells of those who claimed to be disciples but turned away (John 6:66). Although the word is used of believers generally, true or false, and of the twelve apostles, this discussion is about genuine disciples. That is what the Lord had in mind when he addressed the multitudes and invited them to follow Him (Luke 14:25-26).

When we invite people to follow the Lord Jesus we should call them to a path of discipleship. Such a life is voluntary. We should not pressure anyone, just as the Lord did not attempt to coerce people. In the light of Matthew 28:20 we should do more than invite people to know about the Lord, or even just to know the Lord. We should invite them, as He did, to observe or obey *all* that He commanded. Ideally the church should be a fellowship of disciples, not a warehouse of listeners or service attenders. Our purpose is to see spectators transformed into holy, devoted worshipers who are walking and working together with Christ (2 Cor. 6:1).

REQUIREMENTS FOR DEVELOPMENT OF DISCIPLES

Doctrine can be taught to groups, but discipling must be done one-on-one. The two aspects can be separated functionally, but both really should occur at the same time. Discipling requires response or action, while doctrinal teaching often takes place in general groups where this does not happen. It is possible to teach the basic principles that are necessary for making disciples in a few hours. However, it is difficult to establish these principles in people's lives without much personal attention over an extended period of time. Good discipling is a slow work. When it is not done to a high standard of quality, it produces poor results. Here are some important factors.

1. WHAT THE DISCIPLER SHOULD BE

We must be developed in our own character before we have anything worthwhile to share with others. Jesus must be our Lord. We must be subject to Him in every area of our lives, without any conscious reservations. We are not speaking about human perfection, but about true sincerity and an evident progress in our Christian walk.

In doctrinal knowledge and fundamental practices we should have:

A. A good understanding of the Gospel, and the ability to explain it to others.

B. An ability to give a clear testimony; and to live the life which corresponds to our profession of being a follower of the Lord Jesus.

C. A consistent devotional time with God. This includes effective personal application of the Word and a systematic prayer life.

D. Effective dealings with temptation.

E. "Sharing" our faith (witnessing) regularly.

F. An active fellowship in a local church.

G. An ability to work with other believers in harmony (team-work).

H. Freedom from serious character defects which would impair our service or relationships with others.

2. WHAT THE DISCIPLE SHOULD BE

It is important that we pray before agreeing to disciple anyone (Luke 6:12-13). Any person that we choose ought to have a sincere desire to grow in their Christian life and service. He should be faithful (dependable), available (time for regular meetings) and teachable (eager to learn whatever we have to share). There is no inferiority involved in learning anything another person can teach us that is profitable. Some other considerations are :

A. One should be yielded without any reservation, to the Lordship of Christ.

B. One should give a clear testimony, with assurance of salvation, that is consistent with his spiritual life.

C. One should be at a reasonable level of spiritual maturity.

D. One should demonstrate an ability to work in harmony with others.

E. One must be willing to pay the price to grow.

F. One should be willing to help others in the discipling process.

HOW TO WORK EFFECTIVELY AT MAKING DISCIPLES

Disciples are not made by books, manuals, training materials, or courses of study. They are made by other disciples, sharing life to life, what they have learned in the School of God. Discipleship development goes beyond the stage of helping a new believer grow at the initial stage of spiritual life, although beginning principles can be learned here. It is more than remedial Christianity for those already stumbling in their walk, although such help may be needed. It does not have social fellowship or counseling as its **primary** goal. It is a series of serious meetings by serious people seeking to become disciple makers and reproducers for Christ. **All** Christians are "born to reproduce," as was so eloquently stated by Dawson Trotman, founder of the Navigators, an organization which has devoted itself to this ministry for many years. However, not all Christians want to pay the price of becoming a disciple *indeed*, or a **true** disciple (John 8:31). The spiritually eager, those Christians who are ready to give 100%, are the people we need to locate and help grow in this ministry.

How can we implement this goal in a practical way in our assembly? There is no single way, but we can describe an example of how this ministry can function. It must be more than a mechanical duplication of certain steps.

If at all possible, **start with the elders or other leaders,** or at least gain their **full** support. This is something that can only function within a church that has agreed on this ministry as an essential mission. They can meet as a group at first, possibly early in the morning. The leaders, and those who follow, must be committed to mutual **accountability** and **continuous spiritual growth.** The plan is not to do a book study from the Bible, nor to have generalized spiritual talk. It is about fundamental factors in spiritual growth. The session is to follow up each person's own personal time with God in the Word. Each participant should be committed to daily prayer, study, and personal application of Scripture. They should come to the session ready to share from the insight and application which they have received from the Lord that very day.

It should be the goal of the initial core group to expand the chain of contacts to other serious believers, both men and women, so that disciple-making permeates the body. The greatest problem in achieving this goal is that of wise selection and effective training. Meetings which are not high quality or life-changing in character do not reproduce what we seek. The believer who is eager to grow, sacrificial in attitude towards others, as well as devoted to Christ, is the one we seek. Personal appearance, affluence, status, or mere verbal assent to high goals may lead us down the wrong trail in the selection process.

1. The Word as Communication from God. Each person shares from the passage they have studied earlier. They read the text, with perhaps a brief comment. They point out the **spiritual principle** that is evident contextually. They then make a **personal application** that God has laid on their heart. Avoid the trap of generalized comment or agreement. Make it personal, with a corresponding **commitment to take action**. This will give evidence as to whether a person is genuinely hearing the Word of God speaking to him or her. This is essential for spiritual growth. It is developed by practice and by listening to godly people making applications for their lives. It is an example of "iron sharpening iron" (Prov. 27:17).

2. Prayer as an Instrument of Spiritual Warfare. If the weapons of our warfare are not carnal (fleshly) (2 Cor. 10:4), what are they? Certainly our weapons include the sword of the Spirit which is the Word of God (Eph. 6:17). But they also include the amazing privilege of taking our burdens and intercessions to the Lord, knowing that He hears us (1 John 5:15). Effectual prayer does much good (Jas. 5:16b). We should pray aloud together, after reviewing written and oral requests. This draws the participants together in spiritual fellowship. That is one value of exchanging prayer requests. You learn to pray by praying.

3. Witnessing as a Way of Life. We should add the names of unsaved contacts to our prayers lists and prayerfully seek their salvation. This helps our accountability in regular witnessing as we talk about what has been happening in this area. Disciple-making must include witnessing if it is to be realistic and well rounded. It is highly desirable to go together in witnessing opportunities or evangelistic visitation.

4. Sharing from Personal Life and Ministry. We develop deeper levels of fellowship by sharing (in strictest confidence) personal struggles and challenges. We are "REAL" to others when we admit to needs, and seek prayer in these areas. This is a natural outgrowth of sharing what God is saying to us from His Word. An important adjunct to this sharing is to make a written list of personal goals, along specific steps which we plan to take in reaching those goals. This ought to include at least one **character goal** (diligence, steadfastness, courage), one **ministry goal** (improved devotional life, witnessing effectiveness, worship), and one **personal goal** (relationships, finances, etc). These should be written out, and a copy given to the person to whom we have made ourselves accountable. All of this process is voluntary.

5. Memorization of Scripture. This can be very helpful in the mutual accountability between the two persons. Begin with a simple series of gospel verses which are useful in witnessing. Then add key verses which relate to major areas of our walk with God.

The goal of the entire program goes beyond that of helping another believer grow spiritually. It has in view the time when this person will take up the same ministry with another person so as to become a fellow helper in disciple-making. We can continue together as long as growth is evident. We should disengage from these meetings, as gracefully as possible, when it is evident that this growth is not occurring. We are not abandoning them. We are simply recognizing that our meetings have not been sufficiently helpful to justify their continuance. Perhaps they can be resumed at some future date, or another person can do a better job.

We do not claim that the men whom Paul discipled (Timothy, Silas, and others) followed the *exact* plan as outlined above. However, they surely involved many of the same elements. Paul was a spiritual parent to many, as both a father (1 Thess. 2:11) and a nursing mother (1 Thess. 2:7). Obviously he wanted to see them strong in the Word, in prayer, and in continuous growth as disciples.

As this work is diligently carried forward and spreads throughout the church, it will have a profound effect upon corporate spiritual life. It will insure practical assistance for those who sincerely want to be growing disciples and are willing to do whatever is necessary to achieve this.

HINDRANCES TO MAKING DISCIPLES

Unfortunately, not every discipling relationship leads to a successful outcome. The problem may be either with the discipler or the disciple.

1. PROBLEMS FOR THE DISCIPLER

A. A lack of faithfulness in prayer and preparation for your meetings.

B. A lack of sincere personal interest, so the person feels like a project or assignment. A lack of time and availability for the person may be a part of the discipling failure.

C. Breakdown or flaws in your own life are evident, to a discouraging degree. If you become close friends, they may detect unacceptable inconsistency in your life.

D. You may be too demanding without sensitivity to the learner's weaknesses or struggles.

2. PROBLEMS FOR THE DISCIPLE

A. They are not sufficiently committed to the Lord or to the process.

B. They are not listening, not following through, on agreed assignments. Undisciplined life or consistent tardiness is the norm.

C. Excuses, blame-shifting, dwelling on past failures are used to justify lack of progress.

D. There is talk about problems without action taken to correct them.

E. There is failure to obey in areas of which they are well aware.

F. Self-centeredness, rather than being others-directed and Christ-centered is very apparent.

G. Laziness or unwillingness to make needed efforts to improve is evident.

H. There are wrong motives for wanting to meet, such as: to

socialize, to be seen by others as spiritual, to advance in visible areas of service, to just get attention from the discipler.

CONCLUSION AND APPLICATION

It is well to remember that sincere praise, more often than criticism, should be given the one being discipled. It is necessary to give affirmative Biblical and practical help to establish good patterns. The standard must always be God's Word, not your personal opinion. Use the Word frequently. Express love consistently. Listen carefully. Keep your own word in the smallest matter. Above all, be as much like the Lord Jesus as you can, by the enablement of His Spirit. Bear in mind His example in the training of the Twelve.

Discipling is a spiritual endeavor of the highest importance. It deserves our best efforts. Primarily, we can only see others change through prayer, not methods. The rewards of success are enormous, to the church and to the individual for eternity. There is a high personal price paid for doing it well, and it sometimes seems discouraging. However, your labor is far better directed on one disciple than in seemingly endless time spent with many unproductive and unresponsive people. It is a labor to which the Lord Jesus gave a substantial priority in His life. It is worth your time. It is vitally important to the church's spiritual growth.

The Dynamic Church
STUDY GUIDE

THE DISCIPLING OF THE CHURCH LESSON 12

1. From the following verses, what is a genuine disciple, according to the Master?

    Luke 6:40

    Luke 14:26

    Luke 14:27

    Luke 14:33

    John 8:31

    John 13:34,35

2. How do the examples of the builder and the king in Luke 14:28-32 help us to understand what it means to forsake all?

3. What is the difference between *teaching them all things* and *teaching them to observe all things* (NIV, "to obey everything")? (Matt. 28:20) What could be done to improve this in your fellowship?

4. Read Colossians 1:28,29. According to these Scriptures, what is the goal of disciple-making, and how should we accomplish it?

5. Read 1 Thessalonians 1:1-7. What was the Apostle Paul's teaching method? What was the response of his hearers?

6. Read 1 Thessalonians 2:7,8. What kind of relationship should a discipler have to a learner?

7. How would you evaluate your own readiness to be a committed disciple of the Lord, and to be committed to learning *how to live* from a disciple whose life you admire in the church?

8. Is there anything in this lesson that you do not understand?

MISSIONS AND THE CHURCH   LESSON 13

"The field is the world..." (Matt. 13:38).

Missionary vision is an integral part of the Christian faith. Ours is a missionary faith, an evangelizing faith. God has not called us to be only a gathering of people who practice certain ethical, cultural and religious forms. Our Master has told us, "Go into all the world and preach the Gospel to all creation" (Mark 16:15). If that vision grows dim, or disappears, we have lost a view of a central imperative in the teaching of the Lord Jesus. Our mission field is *worldwide*.

There is an urgency in conveying this message as widely as possible. The Lord warned listeners, "He who does not believe has been judged already, because he has not believed in the name of the only begotten Son of God" (John 3:18). Those without Christ are described as having no hope and without God in this world (Eph. 2:12). The Lord came so that whosoever believes in Him should not perish but have everlasting life (John 3:16). It was necessary for Him to come and give up His life so that He might save that which was lost (Luke 19:10). He was the first foreign missionary, coming from Heaven to earth. He came to this wicked place with the loving purpose to save sinners.

His mission of proclamation has been given to His people, the Church of Christ, that we might share it with *the world*. "As the Father has sent me, I also send you," were the words of Jesus to us, His followers (John 20:21). We must lift up our eyes and look on the fields which are white unto harvest (John 4:35). We must not be willing that any should perish, but that all should come to repentance (2 Pet. 3:9). The Church is the pillar and ground of truth (1 Tim. 3:15). Therefore, it must be the mainstay of all missionary endeavor. It must provide the vision, the laborers, the financial means, the prayers and the continuing energy to sustain missionary thrust into every place on earth. The Church has not been authorized by God to delegate this task to other organizations. The Church, with all its local expressions, is founded and commissioned by God as His operational representative on earth. Our local or national efforts at evangelism are insufficient when there is such a worldwide need.

LOCAL CHURCHES AND MISSIONARY WORK

What do we mean by missions and missionaries? A true missionary is a child of God called to work with another people who are without an accurate knowledge of God's salvation, based upon His Word. Missions, especially foreign missions, is the field of endeavor devoted to the task of reaching people in Gospel-deficient areas outside our own community or nation. If the command of Christ to proclaim the Gospel to all nations is still valid, then the issue becomes one of obeying the Lord. If the Church as the people of God is His representative on earth, then the command applies to us. This leaves us with the question, "What shall be the extent of the involvement of my local church in obeying the Lord?"

The history of missions demonstrates that local churches have always been the bases for spreading the Gospel. It began in the Book of Acts. Several writers have called attention to the church in Antioch, a city in Syria, as a model of early missionary vision (Acts 11:19-30; 13:1-4). Paul and Barnabas labored extensively here in teaching and training the many converts. Antioch was a growing and spiritual church, a prerequisite for making an effective contribution to missions. The church had developed a number of good teachers. The Spirit of God moved to have Paul and Barnabas set apart for foreign missionary activity (Acts 13:1-4). The church commended them to this ministry (Acts 14:26). There was no intermediary organization involved in the process. No pledges were solicited for their support, and no guarantees were given. They depended on God, and they had the support of the believers there.

During the first two years, this energetic missionary team established at least four local churches (Antioch in Pisidia, Lystra, Iconium, and Derbe, plus the whole island of Cyprus). They reported back to their home church as people to whom they were accountable (Acts 14:27). No parachurch body (separate organization) intervened in this line of responsibility.

Missionary activity, flowing out from the first local churches, continued for centuries. Unfortunately, there was increasing administrative control of the Christian church by centralized overseers working in administrative centers. This did not always help the cause of genuine missionary work. Partially as a result of such church organizations the thrust of foreign missions grew weaker. Revival came many centuries later when small groups, often persecuted by large official churches, renewed the Biblical vision of reaching out to those without Christ in remote lands. An example of this was the community at Herrnhut, Germany, under the leadership of Zinzendorf. This small group dispatched missionaries to distant places worldwide out of their deep spiritual concern for the lost. Herrnhut's influence persisted for centuries. It is amazing that so much was done by this small community! During the 19th Century there was a great missionary revival rooted in a general spiritual awakening in the English-speaking world. Such renewals seemed always to generate a concern for the lost, including those in foreign countries. God has demonstrated that He will work mightily in any group which has a zeal for reaching those who have not heard the Gospel. Much missionary endeavor was carried on by so-called "independent faith missions" and separate groups, rather than flowing out from local churches.

WORLD NEED AND MISSIONARY WORK

It is comfortable to think that the world is now evangelized and the need for missionaries has now largely passed! If this were so, the Lord would surely have come by now, both to spare the righteous and shut the mouths of the wicked (Matt. 24:14; 2 Pet. 3:3-9). Instead He waits for many more of the Christless multitudes of the world to hear the Gospel and respond. There are more than 5 billion souls at this present hour on this planet. No more than 200 to 300 million are estimated to be born-again believers, although there are over one billion professing Christians. Accept either figure, and it would still leave a staggering number to be reached. Wholesale blocks of people in the hundreds of millions are yet to be reached in Muslim countries, Asia, India, Europe and South America. Some nations do not have a single known believer. Hundreds of linguistic groups have yet to receive even a portion of the Bible in their own language. Sections of western societies are so secularized, or misled by false teaching, that they are as ignorant of the Bible as a heathen tribe in some distant place. The most receptive people in any society are the young. About 50% of some population groups are young people, less than 25 years of age. Some segments of these student populations, or young working classes, have never been penetrated with the gospel. It has been said that the national believers in some countries are responsible to reach their own people through the believers now among them. Yet thoughtful leaders of these nations have declared their need for more missionaries from nations and churches that can send them trained servants of God.

Among the needs on the foreign mission field is the lack of effective leadership training (including practical discipleship); pacesetters in evangelism for the apathetic or intimidated; good literature for the literate; records and cassettes for others; fluent Bible translators and strong workers in student and university centers. Foreign workers need to train nationals and work beside them, then step aside and yield control. Foreign money freely given to nationals often does more harm than good in the long term. Dependency on money and jealousy of workers supported by liberal "foreign money" can have detrimental long-term effects on the national churches and their leadership.

Some have pointed to the frequent rejection of outside missionaries coming into a land. Lately, there have been great difficulties in obtaining visas for foreign entry. Still there are many ways to infiltrate Christian workers into a country without them being designated as missionaries. Difficulties have not prevented the entrance of Catholic priests or other religious workers into many foreign countries. Commercial and technical people, students and visitors jam the airlines to go everywhere in today's "one world" environment. Many countries have opened their doors much wider to entrance by visitors. God uses various methods to reach the peoples of the earth with His gospel.

HINDRANCES TO EFFECTIVE MISSIONARY WORK

The problem does not seem to be a lack of opportunity or need, nor has the Lord changed the great commission for this day. The real problem may be divided under two headings, those in a changing world and those in a weakened church.

In the world there are serious but not insurmountable difficulties.

1. There is a **decline in the belief of spiritual and moral absolutes**. The difference between what is true and false, or right and wrong, is either denied or not perceived. **Relativism** rules. This is the view that an ethical or moral truth is simply a matter of what any group or people choose to believe for themselves because truth has no fixed basis. It has been suggested that since our minds are limited, therefore we cannot be sure that we know anything for certain. So who can say what is right or wrong in any absolute way? This deadly, human view denies the authority of God and His Word.

2. Allied to the view above is **secularism**. This view states that God

is irrelevant to our worldly, time-based living. All that matters in life is living for *now* in this world. Another companion view is **materialism**. This idea suggests that a highest good is obtained by possessing goods or things and satisfying physical or psychological desires. A form of this philosophy is communism. A more subtle form of materialism, and possibly more dangerous, is embraced by believers who live to accumulate possessions at the expense of serving the Lord. At the same time they profess to believe what the Lord Jesus taught. Their lifestyle contradicts their profession of faith.

3. An ever-increasing dangerous viewpoint is **humanism**, including humanistic psychology, seen especially among the educated. In this approach, man is made to be the center for interpreting what is good in life. Humanists do not care for, nor accept, God's plan for their lives. In extreme forms of humanism, man becomes his own god or supreme authority.

4. **False religion**, in an almost infinite variety of forms, continues to grow. It deceives man in his spiritual search for satisfaction and meaning in life by offering a counterfeit to the truth. False prophets and false teachers create elaborate systems of deceit to entrap millions. These religions generate zealous missionaries of their own who are often more active in some places than the advocates of the truth.

5. There is a tremendous tide of **propaganda** directed against the Christian faith and its representatives all over the world. It is growing constantly, especially within the medium of films and television shows. These often depict Bible-quoting madmen, bigots, and deranged ministers as representative of the Christian faith.

The **problems in the weakened church** are the most serious of all. We need to correct these in order to have healthy grassroots expansion of missionary work.

1. There is a **decline in the numbers, quality, and support of missionaries**. In many countries more missionaries are coming back, or retiring, than are going out.

2. There is a **decline in practical belief** in the perilous condition of the lost, and in the urgency of reaching them with the Gospel. Apparently, believers can hold evangelical doctrines, memorize verses and attend churches in considerable numbers, yet live as those who had not the slightest concern for billions without Christ in other places.

3. Believers are not taught to **obey Christ and to follow Him in all His teachings**. They pick and choose the areas in which they will respond. This includes commitment to missions.

4. Affluence and compromise with worldly standards have sapped the spiritual strength of those in the church. **Nominalism**, or being a Christian in name only, is a greater problem than is realized in the evangelical church. There seems little interest in living a sacrificial life for Christ and His Kingdom.

5. There is a growing belief in **universalism**. This is the doctrine that all or at least most of mankind, will be saved in the end by the mercy of God.

6. There is also an increase in **syncretism** which combines non-Christian customs and practices with Biblical elements. They are, in fact, alien to one another. The Scriptures are misinterpreted so that they appear to be compatible with non-Christian ideas. Hearers or readers do not seem to be able to discern this clearly. Merging Christian beliefs with alien elements eliminates the need to evangelize. We just merge with the error.

BASIC CHURCH ACTIONS REQUIRED FOR SUCCESSFUL MISSIONARY WORK

The local church can be a vital force for missionary effort if it commits itself to the task. The beginning step is to become a lively, evangelizing, and discipling church through the reviving work of the Holy Spirit, just as Antioch of Syria did long ago. Lukewarm or apathetic churches are not an effective base for missionary outreach. When some progress has been made on this foundation, there are other needed steps.

1. **Determine** to be a church which sends Spirit-empowered missionaries to the field. When this goal is firmly set, it is more likely to happen.

2. **Raise up** laborers to work in your church, rather than try to import them from outside. Impart a vision for the world. Provide practical training within the church to put believers to work in influencing the lives of others for Christ. Develop a pool of effective workers, so that from this group some can be encouraged to go overseas.

3. **Keep the church abreast** of interesting and timely missionary news concerning workers in whom you are interested. See that the congregation hears challenging messages about the mission field. Establish a special missions prayer group of men and women, meeting regularly to share information about the field, and have them cry out to God for workers.

4. **Encourage and select** proper candidates to go. Perhaps short term exposures during summers, or for a year, will indicate how well they can become accustomed to the mission field, and how well they do while there. Do not send out people for this purpose unless they have given some evidence of fruit of their labor at the home church.

5. **Strengthen** financial support for workers in the field that you know are doing an effective job.

6. **Write letters** to encourage the workers. They delight in receiving these letters and keenly feel their lack. Visit workers when possible to encourage them, to see how well they are doing, and to observe how the church may meet their needs.

CONCLUSION AND APPLICATION

In Revelation 3:8, the Lord Jesus evaluated and challenged the local church at Philadelphia, a city in what is now Turkey. He said, "Behold, I have put before you an open door which no one can shut, because you have a little power and have kept my word."

The Lord has also set before us today, in our churches, an open door of missionary opportunity, and there is great need. Only He can shut that door and He has not yet done so. We have a little power and could have even more, if we were determined to obey His Word, especially in this matter.

In the Old Testament, Jonah refused to go to Nineveh as a missionary despite God's clear command. His disobedience was punished, then his path redirected. The result was a missionary triumph among the Assyrians. God today will bless those churches who hear His call to spread the Gospel throughout the world. Churches are His agents in fulfilling His desire to reach the lost unto the uttermost parts of the earth. Every church will be evaluated by the Lord Jesus, just as was Philadelphia and the other churches of the Scripture. May we not be found wanting in this regard when we are evaluated before the Judgment Seat of Christ.

**The Dynamic Church
STUDY GUIDE**

MISSIONS AND THE CHURCH   LESSON 13

1. What is the goal of the church's work in the world (Luke 24:47)?

2. What does Jesus see, and how does He feel, when He looks at the world (Matt. 9:36)?

3. What does the Lord Jesus instruct us to do in response to His view of the world (Matt. 9:37,38)?

4. What happened to the Apostles after Jesus started them praying for workers to be sent into God's harvest (Matt. 10:1,5-7)?

5. List three ways in which the church at Antioch is a good model for local churches today in assisting the work of missions (Acts 11:20-26; 13:1-4; 14:26-27).

6. In your own words, what is the meaning of:

   relativism

   secularism

   materialism

   humanism

   syncretism

7. Use Acts 14:21-28 to write a clear job description for a missionary.

8. How can you help your assembly make an impact on the task of worldwide missions (Col. 4:2,3; Phil. 4:15-19)?

9. What truth in this lesson most impressed you?

10. Is there anything that you did not completely understand in this lesson?

NOTES

NOTES